OPTIONS
TRADING STRATEGIES

A BEGINNERS' GUIDE TO THE MOST USEFUL TOOLS, STRATEGIES
AND TRICKS TO EARN MONEY WITH OPTIONS TRADING
AND TAKE THE ROAD TOWARDS LONG-TERM PROFITABILITY

NATHAN PRICE

© Copyright 2021 Nathan Price – All rights Reserved

The content contained within this book may not be reproduced, duplicated, or transmitted without direct written permission from the author or the publisher.

Under no circumstances will any blame or legal responsibility be held against the publisher, or author, for any damages, reparation, or monetary loss due to the information contained within this book. Either directly or indirectly.

Legal Notice:

This book is copyright protected. This book is only for personal use. You cannot amend, distribute, sell, use, quote, or paraphrase any part, or the content within this book, without the consent of the author or publisher.

Disclaimer Notice:

Please note the information contained within this document is for educational and entertainment purposes only. All effort has been executed to present accurate, up-to-date, and reliable, complete information. No warranties of any kind are declared or implied. Readers acknowledge that the author is not engaging in the rendering of legal, financial, medical, or professional advice. The content within this book has been derived from various sources. Please consult a licensed professional before attempting any techniques outlined in this book.

By reading this document, the reader agrees that under no circumstances is the author responsible for any losses, direct or indirect, which are incurred as a result of the use of the information contained within this document, including, but not limited to, errors, omissions, or inaccuracies.

Table of Contents

INTRODUCTION 6
- OPTIONS 101 7
- TYPES OF OPTIONS 8
- PURPOSE OF OPTIONS 10
- OPTIONS TERMINOLOGIES 12

CHAPTER 2: WHO THIS BOOK IS FOR? 16
- EVALUATING YOUR PERSONAL FINANCIAL SITUATION 16

CHAPTER 3: WHAT IS THE FUTURE OF TRADING IN THE STOCK MARKET? 22
- PROFITING REGARDLESS OF MARKET CONDITIONS 22

CHAPTER 4: WHAT IS MY APPROACH TO OPTIONS TRADING? 26
- WHICH UNDERLYING ASSETS? 27
- DOING RESEARCH 28
- CENTRAL AND TECHNICAL ANALYSIS 29
- HAZARD AND MONEY MANAGEMENT 30

CHAPTER 5: WHAT ARE THE TOOLS? 32
- THE BROKER 32
- MINIMUM EQUITY REQUIREMENT 36
- DIRECT-ACCESS AND CONVENTIONAL BROKERS 37
- THE TRADING PLATFORM 39
- REAL-TIME MARKET DATA 44
- THE DAY TRADING ORDERS 44

CHAPTER 6: WHICH TECHNICAL INDICATOR DO I OFTEN USE FOR TRADING? ... 46

CHAPTER 7: WHAT KIND OF TRADING STRATEGY ARE SHORT SELLING AND MARGIN TRADING? 52
- SHORT SELLING 52
- UNDERSTANDING MARGIN TRADING 52
- MONEY & RISK MANAGEMENT TECHNIQUES 53
- RISK MANAGEMENT TECHNIQUES 54

CHAPTER 8: HOW HARD CAN THE TRADING POSSIBLY BE? 56
- YOU ARE ABLE TO WEATHER THE STORM 56
- YOU DON'T MAKE EMOTIONAL DECISIONS 56
- BE A LITTLE BIT MATH-ORIENTED 57
- YOU ARE MARKET-FOCUSED 57
- FOCUS ON A TRADING STYLE 57
- KEEP DETAILED TRADING JOURNALS 57
- OPTIONS TRADERS ARE FLEXIBLE 58
- TAKE A DISCIPLINED APPROACH 58

CHAPTER 9: WHAT ARE THE MOST POPULAR OPTIONS TRADING STRATEGIES USED BY HEDGE FUND MANAGERS? 60

Covered Calls 60
Buying and Selling Puts 60
ITM 61
OTM 61
Iron Condor 61
Iron Butterfly 61
Collar Strategy 62
Short Put 62
Long Put 62
Credit Spread 63
Debit Spread 63
Strangles and Straddles 63
Rolling Out Options 64
Options Greeks 64

CHAPTER 10: HOW MANY YEARS DOES IT TAKE TO MASTER OPTIONS TRADING? 66

Avoiding Common Pitfalls in Options Trading 66

CHAPTER 11: HOW CAN I GET ANY BREAKING NEWS EARLIER? 72

Identify the Fastest and Most Effective Strategy 72
Develop a Trading Plan 76

CHAPTER 12: WHAT ARE SOME RULES FOR WRITING COVERED CALLS THAT A TRADER SHOULD ALWAYS FOLLOW? 82

What is an Options Contract on the Stock Market? 82
Call Options 82
Ways to Close an Options Contract 84

CHAPTER 13: STRATEGIES AND TRICKS THAT CAN BE APPLIED 86

Never Think of Dollar Value. Consider a Fixed Percentage 86
Hedge 87
There Has Never Been a "Multi-Purpose" Strategy 87
There is Always an Exit Strategy 87
Conduct Research before Repeating 88
Never Use Cashless Redemption Options (ATM) to Start Trading 88
Options with Poor Trading Liquidity 89
Options Trading Mistakes to Avoid 90

CHAPTER 14: HAS ANYONE MADE ANY SIGNIFICANT MONEY FROM TRADING? 94

The Road to Long-Term Profitability 94

CONCLUSION 98

ABOUT THE AUTHOR 102

Introduction

There are many ways to make your money dynamic. Most people turn to traditional investing, and that's okay. However, the results obtained by investing in traditional stocks are generally quite conservative. Those looking to exit with higher profits are likely to benefit from a more dynamic trading method. Of course, there are several ways to negotiate, and some are new. However, one of the best ways to start a business would be to use a standard methodology. In other words, you want to examine the options trading model.

Many people have heard of the concept of options trading but may not be fully familiar with the process. It is a relatively easy process when explained in detail. For those who are not fully familiar with such definitions, here is an overview of a clear definition of what trading will include:

What is an option? It is a contract to buy or sell an underlying security. The most basic options are shares or funds that are traded electronically. There are other basic products, such as futures or precious metals. However, the vast majority of options will be stocks or ETFs, as these are elements that most people are familiar with.

Again, the key to understanding options trading is understanding the concept of the contract. A contract to promote option trading will set a very specific price called a "price strike." This refers to the actual price at which the contract will be bought or sold when it is exercised and the specific duration. The contract will contain an expiration date, and once the expiration date is reached, the contract itself becomes invalid.

Options are divided into two different parts: call and put options, which both can be bought and sold. Depending on the goals of the investor, you need to choose one of them and then make a decision on the call or put. Different investors will have different goals or risk assessments. So it doesn't sound like a call or a put that is the best. The same could be said for buying versus selling. Different individuals will have different goals they want to achieve. You just need to find a strategy of options that best suits your individual needs.

Of course, the ability to decide between call and put will depend on understanding a more detailed explanation of the real meaning of each concept. Basically, a call means you have the option (rightfully) to buy underlying stocks or ETFs at an agreed strike price. This can be done no later than the deadline. Obviously, you couldn't do that later, as that would undermine the goal of their expiration date. Along with the put option, the main difference would be that it has the potential to sell stocks or ETFs.

There is another open model in this process, and it can be applied whether you are watching a call or a call. In particular, you can sell the option to someone who wants to buy it. Obviously, this should be done sometime before the deadline to allow the buyer enough time to make an effective decision about what to do with the contract when he buys it.

If you choose to let the option contract expire, it will be an invalid contract. There is nothing wrong with this process, although some may have a negative opinion about the expiration of the contract. However, there is nothing wrong with that, assuming that the execution of the contract will not fulfill the expected result. Again, this would be a buyer/seller contract, and the owner should be able to make effective decisions based on personal and professional judgment. You really don't want to execute a contract in such a way that it jeopardizes the most profitable value.

Options 101

In short, an option is a contract between two parties. One party is the buyer, and the other party is the seller. This contract is essentially a promise that one party makes to buy and the other to sell. This promise is formally documented and executed upon completion of the terms. When all goes well, everyone wins. When something goes wrong, someone loses money.

Options are great because they are a means of boosting an investor's portfolio thereby diversifying the usual investment assets. So, in addition to stocks, bonds, exchange-traded funds (ETFs), and commodities, options provide additional exposure to other asset classes.

It's worth noting that options are predominantly based on stocks though any type of asset could be the subject of an options contract. This is important as you could take out options on other assets such as oil, gold, bonds, and so on.

A simple way in which you can make money with these contracts is to buy low and sell high. You can do this by timing the market. By "timing", we mean that you get into an options contract thinking about what the future might hold. So, if you are speculating that the price of an asset will rise or fall, an options contract will have you covered.

Now, the reason why these types of contracts are called, "options" is because they give holders the right to buy or sell but do not generate an obligation. This is why they are used to hedge risk. If a holder deems it appropriate to pull out of a deal, they can do so within the parameters of the contract. An example of this may be a timeframe limitation such as being unable to pull out within 48 hours of the contract's expiration.

Types of Options

There are two main types of options, "calls" and "puts." All other types of options are derived from these two basic types. The terms and conditions of these contracts can vary widely. However, their parameters are limited to time, the number of shares (or quantity of the asset in question), and monetary terms.

For instance, a contract may stipulate that the holder can buy 100 shares of FXY corp. within 72 hours of the contract being issued. The agreed share price is $11.50 per share. The expiration of the contract is one week. As such, the holder can execute the contract within the parameters. However, if they choose to back out, they must notify the other party 24 hours in advance.

In this example, we can see that multiple conditions must be met. When met, the contract can be executed. Otherwise, there may be penalties to pay. Also, please keep in mind that the terms and conditions depend on the market and type of asset being traded.

<u>Call Options</u>

A "call option" provides the holder the opportunity to buy an asset but does not imply an obligation. This is important to note as the holder has the right to pull out of the deal so long as it is within the parameters of the contract.

Let's consider this example:

A car is on the market for $1,000. A prospective buyer looks at it and decides the want to buy it. However, the potential buyer thinks it's too expensive at this price point. The seller won't budge as they hope to get the full price for it.

So, both parties enter into an agreement. The interested buyer is willing to pay $850 for it. The seller thinks they can get a better deal and is willing to wait. So, they agree that if the seller does not make a deal within a month, they will sell to this buyer at $850.

Now, the seller believes they can sell the car before then. But this contract gives them the assurance that if they can't sell the car, they already have a buyer lined up. The buyer is interested in the car but is not desperate. They are willing to wait. If the seller makes a deal before the end of the month, then the buyer does not get the car.

In this example, one month goes by, the seller has no luck, so the holder of the contract (the buyer) executes the contract. The seller is paid $850 and the car changes ownership. That's a fairly straightforward deal.

Put Options

A "put option" is the opposite of a call option. A put allows the holder to sell but not the obligation to do so. In this regard, the seller controls the execution of the contract. As such, puts are used to lock in a sale price particularly when there is uncertainty regarding market conditions.

Let's take a look at an example.

The same individual has the same car up for sale. This time though they get multiple offers from several buyers. Naturally, the seller is looking to find the best deal they can get. One buyer is particularly motivated and has offered to pay the full $1,000. However, the seller thinks they can get a better deal. So, the seller takes on a put option. In this option, the conditions state that the seller will agree to the sale of the car for $1,000 within one week.

Over the next few days, another interested party shows up and is willing to pay $1,200 for the car. The seller makes the deal and subsequently cancels the contract. This is perfectly fine so long as they don't violate any of the stipulations.

The main objective of the put option, in this case, is to protect against a sudden market drop. For instance, both buyer and seller have agreed to a certain price beforehand. So, the seller is protected in the event that car prices drop. The buyer would then be stuck with a car that costs more than it's worth.

This is who options are used to hedge against risk.

Purpose of Options

Options have several purposes. That is why it's important to get to know them as each purpose can provide you with potential income opportunities. You can dabble in one, or all of them, depending on your strategy.

Let's take a look at each one in greater depth.

Speculation

Speculation is about predicting the future. Since no one knows what will happen with certainty, the best we can hope for is to speculate what could happen at some point down the road. The way speculation works are that you anticipate that a stock's price (or any other asset's price) will go up or down. So, you take out an option to play that potential fluctuation.

For example, you wish to buy stock in GHB Company. However, you feel that the stock price will fall within the next couple of weeks. So, you take out a call option with the price parameter set at a lower point. When that price point is triggered, the deal goes through.

To take this to another level, you simultaneously take out a put anticipating that the price will rebound. When that occurs, you buy low and sell high. In the end, you keep the difference or the "spread". The great part is that when you play these types of deals, you don't need a lot of upfront investment capital.

Hedging

The term "hedging" is investment lingo for "protection". When you hedge your portfolio, you have the means to ensure that the value of your investments doesn't get wiped out. For example, you take outputs on your stock holdings in anticipation of a market drop. So, if the market drops, then your holdings are sold off to other investors. This protects you from getting hammered by market fluctuations.

Shorting Stocks

"Shorting" stocks is an advanced use of options, but a highly profitable one. When you short a stock, you essentially sell something you don't own... yet. In this type of deal, you pledge to sell a stock to the buyer before you own it. When the buyer goes through with the purchase, you must then beat the clock to procure the number of shares the buyer paid you for.

This is where options come into play. They can be used to automate this process.

For instance, you have a put option for SDG Company. You sell 100 shares at $11.15 each. So, the buyer executes the contract and pays you $1,115. At the same time, you have a call option for 100 shares of SDG Company at $11 a share. You find a seller at that price point, you execute your call, and voila, you have just made $115 in profits.

This operation sounds simple. However, you need to be aware of how the market is moving. If you time things incorrectly, you'll end up buying the stock at a higher price point thereby causing you to lose money. In the worst of cases, shares of that particular company may dry up. So, even if you have the money to purchase, there are no shares to buy.

<u>Valuating an Option</u>

Time is the most important factor in determining the value of an options contract. In short, the longer a contract does without being executed, the less that it's worth. This is called "time decay." Time decay is a function of the time that a contract has left before expiry. So, the closer a contract get to expiration, the less that it's worth. Some investors are specialists at searching for contracts close to expiry as they can be the source of great bargains. Based on this concept, an option that expires in one year is worth much more than one that expires in a week. The reason for this is that the longer that's left on a contract, the greater the likelihood that the stock's price will change. This enables investors to recoup their investment.

For instance, if a contract's face value is $1,000, but expires within a week, its real value may be $100 due to time decay. This might seem unfair. However, it helps to think of options like the food at the supermarket. When food items get close to their expiration date, the supermarket may choose to slash its price.

Why?

The supermarket would rather sell the items at cost, or even take a small loss on them, rather than throw away a bunch of items.

The same goes for options.

So, it's important to keep time decay in mind at all times. It's best to think of options at a hot potato. You want to get rid of them as fast as you can. After all, time decay may zap the profits that you stand to make.

Options Terminologies

To familiarize yourself with the alternatives market, it's miles important to understand the basic options terminology.

An option is an agreement that offers the holder the right (i.e. can pick out to), but not the duty (i.e.; no longer have to), purchase or sell a set quantity of stocks, on or earlier than a given date. This proper may be exercised if the holder wishes to or now not because the case can be if it isn't always within the holder's hobby to do so. The holder of the options might best use that right while the fee of the options actions beyond the fixed "workout fee" plus the cost of the option, then the option may be bought at a profit, or it could be exercised. If not, since there may be no duty to exercising the proper, the option can be left to expire, and the client could forfeit his premium (or fee of the option). An option is more precious the similarly away, it's far to the expiry date since there's a greater opportunity of a profitable motion of the underlying proportion as there may be more time for the underlying share to move. This component of the options is known as time price, so the extra the time to expiry, the extra the time value of the options. The closer to the expiry, the lesser the time value of the options.

Premium

Since the Options themselves don't have a crucial worth, the Options premium is the cost that you need to pay to buy options. The bonus is controlled by way of exceptional components, which includes the hidden stock cost, unpredictability inside the market, and the days until the Option's termination. In alternatives replacing, selecting the top rate is one of the most substantial segments.

Fundamental Asset

In alternatives exchanging, the vital useful resource can be stocks, fates, records, items, or money. The fee of Options gotten from its structural support. The Option of capital gives the privilege to buy or sell the stock at a particular fee and date to the holder — subsequently, its miles about the hidden aid or stocks on the subject of Stock in Options Trading.

Lapse Date

In alternatives replacing, each investment possibility has a termination date. The termination date is moreover the hold going date on which the Options holder can exercise the privilege to buy or sell the Options which are in holding. In Options Trading, the termination of Options can shift from weeks to months to year's contingent to be had and the guidelines.

Alternatives Style

There are two extensive styles of Options that are drilled in the considerable majority of the alternatives changing markets.

It is crucial to realize the Options before you begin changing Stock Options. A lot of alternatives exchanging methodologies are performed around the option.

It characterizes the relationship between the strike price of an option and the present price of the underlying Stocks. We will analyze every period in detail beneath.

Purchasing, Selling Calls/Puts

There are four things you may do with options:

- Purchase calls
- Sell calls
- Purchase puts
- Sell puts

Purchasing stock offers you a prolonged position. Purchasing name alternatives provide you with a lengthy capacity view inside the hidden percentage. Short promoting a stock gives you a quick look. Selling a bare or found outcall gives you a likely brief position in the underlying stock.

Purchasing a placed opportunity gives you a brief capacity position within the underlying stock. Selling a stripped or unmarried, however, gives you a probable long place within the hidden stock. Keeping these 4 situations straight is considerable.

Individuals who purchase alternatives are referred to as holders, and the individuals who sell alternatives are called authors of alternatives. Here is the important qualification amongst holders and authors:

- Call holders and put holders (customers) are not committed to purchase or promote. They have the selection to exercise their privileges. This restricts the risk of clients of alternatives to simply the top rate spent.

- Call pupils and put authors (venders), in any case, are committed to purchase or sell if the opportunity lapses in-the-cash (greater on that underneath). This implies a merchant is probably required to follow thru on an assured to buy or sell. It additionally indicates that opportunity dealers have a creation to additional, and sometimes, boundless, dangers. This implies essayists can lose drastically more than the fee of the alternative's premium.

Writer

For every holder of options, there ought to be a person who takes the alternative position. When an option client buys the proper but not the duty in a settlement, it follows that the man or woman on the other aspect of the transaction has to expect the obligation but no longer the proper.

This individual is known as the "writer". The creator takes on the duty to make delivery of the underlying stock if the holder sporting activities his name and takes transport of stock inside the case of a positioned. For assuming his obligations, the writer gets paid a premium i.e.; the price that the purchaser pays for. The alternative top rate is determined not handiest from the call for and supply but also close to variables together with time remaining till expiry, a charge of the underlying stocks, relative to the workout, or strike charge of the options.

Other factors include dividends at the underlying stocks, interest rates, and volatility. The top rate is commonly determined by way of the buyers and sellers but usually similar to the theoretical rate as devised with the aid of numerous mathematical models, including Black Scholes or binomial distribution. Such a software program is to be had and a search on the internet needs to display such models.

Exercise

Exercise within the economic context is the use of the proper via the option holder to purchase the stocks at exercising price if the option is a name, or to promote the underlying shares at the exercise charge if the option is a put.

When a name is exercised, the writer of the option is obliged to make shipping of the underlying stocks on the workout fee, and the holder of the alternative must take transport of the stocks.

When a put is exercised, the author needs to take transport of the underlying stocks on the workout rate, and the holder of the option is obliged to make shipping.

Theory

The idea is a guess on destiny cost bearing. An examiner might imagine the price of a stock will go up, maybe established on essential examination or specialized investigation. An examiner may also buy the stock or purchase a naming opportunity on the stock. Estimating with a name option — in preference to shopping for the stock internal and out — is beautiful to unique dealers since alternatives give influence. Out-of-the-cash call alternatives may just cost a couple of dollars or even pennies contrasted with the maximum of a $100 stock.

Supporting

Alternatives have certainly been concocted for supporting purposes. Supporting other alternatives is supposed to lower the danger at a realistic expense. Here, we cannot forget to utilize picks like a safety arrangement. Similarly, as you safeguard your home or vehicle, alternatives may be used to shield your ventures against a downturn.

Envision that you need to buy innovation stocks. Be that because it may also, you likewise need to restrict misfortunes. By using positioned alternatives, you can limit your downside danger and appreciate all the upside in a financially savvy way. For brief sellers, call alternatives can be used to restrict misfortunes assuming incorrectly — particularly for the duration of a moderate crush.

CHAPTER 2:

Who This Book is for?

This book is perfect for self-driven investors where essential topics are covered giving you the confidence to get started in your trading journey. Although this book is only a small slice of all you can learn about options trading, it's a great introduction to the world of trading. I also encourage you to learn more about the intricacies and the complexities of each financial instrument that you are interested in trading. You should also continue exploring the best strategies so you can find this career worthy of your time and talent. Whether you are trading using a small or a large account, discipline is the key to success. If you can't stick to your strategy, it is better to try something else. Most traders have failed in day trading because of their lack of discipline. It is by being disciplined that you will know when to enter and exit the market. With discipline, you will also understand the importance of using only one percent of your trading capital.

Evaluating Your Personal Financial Situation

There are many ways to go about investing and knowing which path to take can be a daunting process. You can narrow down the possibilities to a strategy that works for you by evaluating your current financial situation. This should be done before you enter your first trade. To be successful, an investor needs a clear picture of where they are going. Keep in mind this is not a one-time event. You should reevaluate your financial situation on an annual basis since it's going to be changing. When you find yourself in a different financial situation, your investment strategies will change over time.

Where Are You Now?

Establishing a starting point is the first step. You don't have to be a financial wizard, but you need to be aware of your present situation before jumping in and buying stocks. Consider the following scenario. An investor, with a large personal debt that has an interest rate of 17%, keeps putting money in the stock market, hoping to build wealth over time. That sounds reasonable, but most market returns are going to be in the range of 5-10%. That means that someone in this situation is losing money.

Seek Liquidity

We are going to recommend that you look for assets you can sell. The money can be used to pay debts, back taxes, or seed investment capital. You'll want to list all of your assets by liquidity, which means how easily they can be converted into cash. You'll also want to consider how much cash you can raise by selling each item if you were to sell it. A house might have a lot more value than a television set, but you might sell the television set in 24 hours while you'd have to wait months to sell the house.

Dealing with Debts

Taking care of debts is one of the first things that a budding investor needs to do. While you might be anxious to get started with a large-scale investment plan, if you have debts to take care of you, might want to put it off. So, the first step in preparing your investment plan is to create a simple balance sheet. You don't have to be an accountant, and you're only doing this for yourself, but it needs to be honest and accurate.

You're going to want to put together a listing of all of your assets and liabilities. When compiling assets, you should include everything of value that you could sell. This could be a computer that you're not using, a dusty TV in a room nobody goes into very often, or an old guitar. Selling things, you don't need can help you pay off debts faster and raise investment capital. You might object that you wouldn't raise much money but imagine having an extra $500 to $1,000 to start with.

When listing your liabilities, you're going to want to know how much debt you have, what the interest rates are, and what your monthly payments are. Monthly payments are less important than interest rates. Once you've listed all of your debts, you'll want to develop a plan to pay them off in a reasonable amount of time. There are many calculators available online, and you can also read many records on how to pay off debt. The series of paperwork by debt guru Dave Ramsey is highly recommended.

You can use this calculator to figure out how long it will take to pay off a debt for a given monthly payment. You can enter the interest rate and the time frame you would like along with the monthly payment you're willing to make. Start with the current minimum payment to determine the time required to pay off the debt and work up from there.

In this example, we considered a $21,000 debt with a high 11% interest rate. Paying $450 a month would take five years to pay off the debt.

That isn't a good situation to be in – do you want to saddle yourself with a $21,000 debt for five years?

When you have listed all of your debts, then you can prioritize them. To make the most progress in the shortest amount of time, it can be helpful to tackle the smallest debts first. This not only helps you get rid of your debt faster, but it will also have psychological benefits as you improve your financial situation.

If you have back taxes, you should make these a priority. The reason is that the government tacks on lots of fees and penalties, and if the tax debt is allowed to sit around, it can grow substantially in size. Get payment plans arranged to take care of these debts before they become unmanageable.

Take a look at your spending habits. Having material goods now isn't important if you're planning to become a successful investor. You will be able to buy that BMW or Mercedes you want earlier when you can afford it. For now, your focus should be on being able to direct your financial resources into your investments, so that you can grow your wealth over time. Expensive toys, like a new car, can be a large financial drain. If you have car loans, consider getting out of the car and into a used car that is reliable but costs a lot less. From this point forward, don't use debt to finance purchases. Keep a credit card on hand for emergencies, but don't use it to buy things like records or groceries that should be paid for using cash. If you can't pay for something with cash, it can wait.

__Having an Emergency Fund__

Life is never fair, and we are all going to encounter emergencies. Recent studies have shown that most Americans don't have enough cash on hand to pay a $500 bill. If you are in that situation, you need to rectify it before you jump in with a large-scale investment plan. Remember that paying off debt first is always the priority. Debt is a sink that sucks important financial resources down the drain that could be used for other purposes. However, it's important to start putting money away for an emergency fund to be prepared for the unexpected – and being able to pay for it without having to take on more debt. Or worse, getting into a situation where you can't get credit, but still need to find money to pay emergency bills. Set aside a small amount of money that you can start depositing into a savings account that you won't touch unless there is an emergency. Over time, the goal should be to have enough cash on hand to take care of emergency bills ranging up to $5,000 and to have funds on hand to cover times when you might be unemployed.

Consider Additional Sources of Income

If you have a large amount of debt or find yourself in a situation where coming up with a significant amount of money to invest is difficult, you should consider taking action to increase your income. There are many paths to consider. You can start by looking for a higher paying job. Alternatively, you can look into taking a second job, at least until you are in a better financial situation. Another approach that can be used is to either take on "gigs" or short-term contract work. This can be done online or by doing some side work with companies like Uber. You can even look into starting your own online business to generate more income. This doesn't have to be a permanent situation, but you are going to want to get to a place where you are debt-free and can put $1,000 or more into the stock market every month.

Convert Debts from High Interest to Low Interest

If possible, you should refinance your debts to get lower interest rates. Consider the preceding example, a high interest $21,000 debt that would take five years to pay off. If you could get a lower interest rate, you could shave off months or even years from the debt, while requiring you to put in less overall capital. Getting a secured debt can help as well. A secured debt is a lower risk for the lender, so they will offer lower interest rates. That means you will be able to get out of debt faster.

Net Worth and Changes Over Time

When you've gathered everything together, you'll want to determine your net worth. You are doing this for yourself, so don't be embarrassed if it's in a bad position right now. Simply add up the total current value of your assets and liabilities and subtract the total value of the liabilities from the total value of your assets. This is your net worth. If you can compare the value of each asset now to the value it had at the beginning of the year; you can also calculate the change in your net worth in percentage terms.

Are You Ready to Invest?

If you are debt-free or have a plan in place to take care of your debts and to build an emergency fund, you are ready to begin investing. The first rule of investing is never to invest more than you can afford to lose. If you go about your investment plan carefully, the chances of losing everything are slim to none. Being that said, it's a wise approach to invest as if that could happen. So you shouldn't be investing the following month's house payment or your kid's college funds in the hopes of gaining returns. After you have taken care of your debts and emergency fund, add up all of your basic living expenses, so you know how much you need per month. Anything leftover above that is the amount of money you can invest for now.

Determining Your Financial Goals

Once you are in a position to invest something – even if you can only put in $100 a month now because you're paying off large debts – it's time to sit down and figure out your financial goals. There are several things to keep in mind:

- Age: Generally speaking, the older you are, the more conservative you should be in your investment approach. The reason for this is simple. When things go badly, it takes time to recover and get back on the road to profitability. The older you are, the less time you have to grow your wealth in the future. That means a market crash, or a bad investment has larger consequences than it would have if you had thirty years to recover. Financial advisors generally recommend that older investors put their money in safer investments, which means putting some money into bonds and safe investments like US Treasuries that preserve capital. In the stock market, the older investor will seek out more stable companies that are larger, and while they may be growing, they have slow and steady growth with lower levels of risk. Of course, age can cut both ways. Many people reach their fifties with little to no savings or investment. If that describes your situation, you're going to want to invest more aggressively to seek rapid growth. Younger people also want to invest more aggressively, as they have a time horizon that permits taking on more risk. But the time horizon isn't the only factor if you have no capital to protect; you want to be more aggressive.

- Your financial situation: Are you broke? If so, you might need to think small, investing a little bit at a time. At the same time, you might want to take an aggressive approach, buying high growth stocks that can help you build wealth faster. On the other extreme, if you have a large amount of cash available, you're probably going to want to seek out investments that provide returns while protecting your capital.

You might have heard about options in the past but perhaps never really got too much into them. If you have heard of the stock market or are familiar with the way the stock market works, then you will find that options are rather straightforward.

CHAPTER 3:

What Is the Future of Trading In The Stock Market?

The use of options allows you to predict the future. In this regard, you can protect yourself against a fall in prices, or cash in on a booming market. Either way, you can use options to keep you in the game. Options are a much better alternative to the "buy and hold" strategy as this strategy takes a long time to bear significant fruit. Of course, you can combine the buy and hold strategy with other investment options. In the end, the more money you can invest, the better your chances of making significant returns.

Also, please bear in mind that current market pricing that is today's valuation is a reflection of what investors think will happen at some point in the near future. This implies that markets try to price the future today. If investors feel the market will tank tomorrow, they won't wait until it does. They'll sell today in hopes of anticipating the market's next movements. Therefore, keeping an eye on today's valuation will give you a fairly accurate assessment of what you can expect in a rather short time frame.

Moreover, never forget that markets can turn on a dime. As such, you can't be entirely safe in what investors are thinking. You need to keep your eyes on the ball. Otherwise, falling asleep at the wheel can cause you to miss out on significant opportunities.

Profiting Regardless of Market Conditions

If you're familiar with the stock market, you are aware of how stocks can fluctuate significantly over time. In particular, markets can turn on a dime. They are completely unpredictable and there is no way of telling when shifts can happen. Unless you have a crystal ball, you have no way of determining what can happen.

Of course, investors use analytics tools to help them determine trends. Trends the directions in which individual stocks, or entire markets, are heading. When you learn to read these trends, you can determine with a fair bit of accuracy what may or may not happen. Still, shifts are unpredictable and nearly impossible to time.

A good analysis will lead to you figure out what's coming up further down the road. What you may not be able to do is determine when it's going to happen. So, what you can do is to set yourself up for when the time comes. In this regard, you can take the necessary steps to be ready for whatever may come your way. Seasoned investors come to learn that making money can happen in any market situation. This is something that regular investors aren't fully aware of. You see, traditional financial advisors will tell you that you make money when the markets are up, and you lose money when markets are down. This statement is true if you base your portfolio on current market valuation. In that case, you can get wiped out when the markets take a downturn.

This is why the "buy and hold" strategy isn't always the most successful one.

In the "buy and hold" strategy, you essentially purchase stock, keep it, and then sell it at some point in the future. This strategy is good when you have time on your side. In particular, it works when you have the opportunity to put money into an investment account such as a mutual fund or a 401(k). Then, you have the luxury of waiting 20 or even 30 years before you need to touch the money. But when you invest with the express purpose of making as much money as you can, the buy and hold strategy won't cut it. This is why seasoned investors know that options are the way to make money regardless of the prevailing market conditions.

So, let's take a look at the two main types of market conditions.

Bull Market

You have surely heard the phrase thrown around the media regularly. A "bull market" is termed when the general trend in stock prices is on the rise. In these circumstances, the majority of stocks are up. Of course, this doesn't mean that all stocks are rising across the board. Still, the overall trend is a positive one.

In a bullish market, investors are optimistic. So, they are more inclined to investing money. Furthermore, they may be more inclined to take a greater risk as the market provides room for this. In short, a bullish market is a highly positive trading environment. Investment accounts such as mutual and index funds increase the valuation. If an investor chooses to sell their holdings at this time, they will most likely make a profit.

It's worth noting that more investors buy during a bull market. As such, it's a "seller's market."

Bear Market

The opposite of a bull market is a "bear market." A bear market is when the general trend in stock valuation is downward. In other words, prices are going down as a result of the selloff most investors engage in. It makes sense to visualize an increased sales volume as falling prices motivate investors to dump their holdings before they begin to seriously lose money. When selling begins to take off, prices fall even further.

At this point, most financial advisors tell their customers to "ride out the drop." This makes sense if you have the luxury of time. This means that dips in market valuation can recover. However, there is no telling how long that might take. Some companies never recover from substantial dips in the market.

Most analysts declare a bear market when stock prices fall 20% from a previous high. However, the media is very careful to declare a bear market as such statements can lead investors to panic further fueling the selloff.

CHAPTER 4:

What is My Approach to Options Trading?

A key piece of alternatives exchanging is centered on discovering chances to make exchanges. There are various ways that you can recognize and survey such chances, and we have given data on what is engaged with the procedure. To be effective in your exchange, you will have a lot of chances for exchanges, so this is unquestionably something you should submit some opportunity to.

On the off chance that you have been perusing this guide so as to assist you with beginning with alternatives exchanging, you will thoroughly understand the underlying readiness required and how to pick a merchant. You'll additionally have a comprehension of exchanging levels and how they can influence your capacity to utilize certain procedures. At this stage, it's an ideal opportunity to begin pondering how you are going to discover chances to exchange. You could know totally everything there is to think about choices exchanging, however, such information is just valuable in the event that you can really try everything and recognize chances to make a few benefits.

Despite the fact that alternatives exchanging are actually very perplexing, anybody that is set up to invest energy learning the subject can eventually be effective. Be that as it may, realizing how to exchange alternatives isn't sufficient without anyone else; you have to realize how to bring in cash out of it. This takes difficult work and responsibility since; you should invest the necessary exertion so as to locate the correct chances and afterward make the proper exchanges.

In the event that you can do that reliably, at that point you will very likely accomplish your objectives. On this page, we take a gander at how you approach distinguishing possibly beneficial open doors for exchanging choices.

1. Which Underlying Assets?

2. Doing Research

3. Central and Technical Analysis

Which Underlying Assets?

Despite the fact that choices contracts are resources themselves, they are really subordinating that get their incentive from the hidden resources which they identify with. Choices agreements can be purchased and sold on a wide scope of basic resources that incorporate stocks, remote monetary forms, wares, and lists.

This makes choices exchanging a truly adaptable type of contributing in light of the fact that, you can make speculations on a wide range of monetary instruments just by purchasing and selling choices contracts. This implies one of the principal things you have to consider whenever you are searching for potential choices exchanging openings is actually which of these money related instruments you need to incorporate.

It ought to be evident that you don't have to choose to exchange just investment opportunities, or just forex choices, or just file alternatives. You can purchase and sell the same number of various sorts of choices as you feel great with. Be that as it may, you do need to consider how you will be examining potential exchanges and how you'll be recognizing appropriate chances.

On the off chance that you concluded that you would think about a wide range of various hidden protections, at that point you would be giving yourself the most obvious opportunity with regards to discovering openings due to the wide scope of conceivable outcomes. You should be readied, however, to complete a great deal of investigation into various money related markets which could be very tedious, and it could really make it exceptionally hard to locate the number of chances as you might want.

On the other hand, on the off chance that you concluded that you were just going to exchange investment opportunities dependent on stocks in a specific division, at that point you would have the option to concentrate your examination explicitly on publicly recorded organizations that work around there. You may wind up turning into a specialist in that field and be significantly more adroit at distinguishing related open doors dependent on this skill.

The drawback, obviously, to adopting such a restricted strategy is, that you might be passing uploads of different open doors in various segments and markets that you aren't in any event, taking a gander at.

There truly is no correct way, or incorrect way, to move toward this part of distinguishing openings and we wouldn't offer particular guidance in such a manner.

All we would recommend is that you set aside the effort to consider which fundamental resources you need to incorporate and afterward it's eventually down to what you feel great with and what you think will give you the most obvious opportunity with regards to progress.

On the off chance that you do have solid information about a specific segment or market, at that point it would bode well to use that information, however, there is likewise nothing amiss with taking a more extensive view either. You may conclude that you would prefer not to inquire about and investigate the fundamental resources of alternatives yet would prefer to contemplate the value developments of the choices contracts themselves and exchange in like manner.

Doing Research

The coming of the plan and online innovation has influenced exchanging and interest in more than one way. Not just has it brought about online dealers, which make the entire procedure of purchasing and selling monetary instruments a lot simpler, it has additionally made data identifying with money related instruments significantly more open.

The web gives a for all intents and purposes boundless flexibility of data that can be utilized to look into purposes, and this truly is significant to financial specialists. It's fundamental to begin checking the trades to get modern statements and to follow universal news that can influence the business sectors. In any event, getting money related reports on publicly recorded organizations is something essential to do. The web is a rich wellspring of realities, measurements, and figures that can help gigantically.

Obviously, gathering data is just a single piece of doing research for exchanging purposes. The genuine aptitude is in comprehending what data to search for and afterward realizing how to decipher it. This is an ability in itself, yet it's an expertise that can be effortlessly evolved after some time with a lot of training.

In the event that you are set up to commit a not too bad measure of time to do research and breaking down what you discover when you truly will give yourself a greatly improved possibility of progress with regards to finding conceivably beneficial chances.

Central and Technical Analysis

Central investigation and specialized examination are the two principle strategies utilized by speculators and brokers to break down data and help figure out what exchanges and ventures to make. In spite of the fact that they are both basically utilized for a similar reason, they are altogether different in the manner in which they are utilized.

An essential examination is fundamentally about gathering however much data as could reasonably be expected identifying with particular security and afterward dissecting that data to decide the genuine estimation of that security and how it identifies with its exchanging cost.

For instance, on the off chance that you need to do a central investigation on a stock in a specific organization, at that point you would consider various parts of that organization, for example, their current money related quality, their profit reports, the nature of their administration workforce, and their serious edge in the commercial center. By doing this, you could get a thought of whether the stock was underestimated, exaggerated, or estimated directly comparable to its actual worth. This is to some degree improved, yet it gives you a thought of how essential investigation is utilized.

A specialized investigation is based on utilizing past information to foresee future developments. It includes considering and dissecting outlines and diagrams delineating cost and volume, with the end goal of discovering designs that could uncover patterns that are probably going to be rehashed. The hypothesis is that by following those patterns you can make precise estimates about how security is going to move in cost over a given period of time. Once more, this is a genuinely streamlined perspective on specialized examination, yet it's a sensible outline of what is included.

Both basic examination and specialized investigation are commonly utilized by speculators in stocks, however, they have their utilization in alternatives exchanging as well. The general thought is that you would utilize these strategies to assist you with getting a thought of how you would anticipate that the cost of money related instruments should move, and afterward exchange the fitting alternatives agreements to profit by those moves.

Neither principal investigation nor specialized examination can truly be viewed as better than the other one as there are various variables to consider. Somewhat it boils down to individual inclination; in the event that you feel increasingly good utilizing one of the procedures for your examination, or have a specific fitness for it, at that point it clearly bodes well to utilize that strategy. You may like to utilize a mix of both or utilize key investigation in certain conditions and specialized examination in others.

It merits noting, however, that choices exchanging is frequently about exploiting transient value developments as opposed to whatever else. A crucial examination can assist you with increasing comprehension of the innate worth of security, and it is usually utilized by long haul financial specialists to put resources into underestimated stocks that ought to go up in cost after some time. Be that as it may, it doesn't really assist you with foreseeing value developments in the prompt term.

A specialized examination can, which is the reason choices dealers are most likely bound to profit by utilizing specialized investigation: especially those utilizing a day exchanging style and making a few transient exchanges regularly.

Something else to consider when you are recognizing potential exchanges is how much capital is required and how much hazard is included. Dealing with your spending plan and your introduction to hazard is a significant piece of alternatives exchanging.

Hazard and Money Management

Great administration of your introduction to chance and your exchanging capital is totally crucial in any type of exchanging on the off chance that you can bring in cash over the long haul. There are various techniques you can use for overseeing hazards and controlling your spending plan, for example, utilizing choices spreads and position estimating; our article on hazard and cash the board covers a few of the best ones. We additionally offer guidance on the most proficient method to utilize them.

Effectively dealing with your capital and hazard introduction is basic when exchanging choices. While the chance is basically unavoidable with any type of venture, your introduction to chance doesn't need to be an issue. The key is to deal with the hazard reserves viably; consistently guarantee that you are OK with the degree of hazard being taken and that you aren't presenting yourself to unreasonable misfortunes.

OPTIONS TRADING STRATEGIES

CHAPTER 5:

What Are the Tools?

The main tools you'll need for day trading are an online broker and an order execution platform. You'll also need a very good internet connection and a computer on which to execute your trades on the platform. And if you're not part of a day trading community yet, you'll also need a stock scanner.

The Broker

You'll need a very good broker, who'll be your access to the securities market you plan to day trade in, e.g., the stock market. Take note that your broker can't just be good: it has to be very good. Why?

Since you can't access the stock market or other securities markets directly, you'll need to go through a broker. Even if you choose your SIPs correctly, you can still lose money in your trades if your broker's slow to execute your order at your target price or if their system suffers from frequent glitches.

It can be challenging to choose a broker because there are many of them out there. Some offer top service but are expensive, while some charge very low fees, but their service is crappy. Worse, some are both expensive and crappy!

Factors When Choosing a Broker

1. The standard of the trading software. For online traders, this is the most basic issue, and it takes various inquiries to decide exactly what number of features is incorporated — and how great they are. These include:

- Is the software user-friendly; easy to comprehend and simple to utilize?

- Can I get it on a disk, or would I be able to download it from the internet?

- Is it hard to install on my PC? Will I require help?

32 | P a g .

- Does it require any unique equipment or communications highlights, for example, high-speed modems, specialty internet browsers, or DSL lines — with the end goal to make it work proficiently?

- Does it incorporate adequate pricing and logical, analytical tools for my requirements?

- If not, is it built to be effortlessly incorporated into independent quotation frameworks and analytical services? Let us assume this is the case, are there any exceptional pricing plans?

- Is satisfactory customer documentation given — both printed and online — to enable both to understand the framework and manage any technical issues?

- Is it attractive to look at — and, in the event that I do not like it, would I be able to change such things as size or color, or display? (This may appear to be unimportant, yet in case you will be an active trader, you might take a look at it on and off for six or seven hours every day. In this manner, you do not need something you hate on a stylish premise.)

2. The simplicity of order entry and the speed of transmission to the trade. This is additionally critical for active traders, who might put in heaps of requests and need the procedure to be as programmed as possible. Some key things to ask:

- What number of fields on the order-entry screen do I need to fill in to put in a request?

- Do I really need to type in all the data, or will the software import it from the logical or pricing screens in the event that I need it?

- Do I need to manually go back to the firm's order screen, or would I be able to get to it by tapping on the screens given by incorporated trading partners?

- Does the program send the order to the trade when I submit it, or does it need to be prepared elsewhere inside the firm first?

- Do I need to indicate the trade where the order is sent, or does the program shop around at the best cost and course the order as needs are?

- Do I put orders specifically through your software, or must I have a browser to get to your framework?

- Can orders be entered at night-time, for execution the next day — or just while the market is open?

- Do you additionally have a site — and, provided that this is true, would I be able to put orders from the site and also through the software?

3. Quality of service to options traders. Still another area where you have to make a few important inquiries, including:

- Are there independent order screens for stocks and options?

- If not, can the order screen be personalized to consider options traders?

- Are the options quotes given in the order screen constantly or deferred?

- In the event that you call up an option chain; is it a real-time preview, or a delayed collation of last prices? Furthermore, is it spread out in an orderly way, or do you need to search for the option you need?

- Does the option-pricing framework give you access to current bids and offers, or simply last trading prices? What about volume numbers? Open interest?

- Does the framework include multi-option strategies, for example, spreads, and give you a chance to order them as a unit?

- If so, does it charge one commission for such orders — or survey fees for every option in the combination?

- Do any of the incorporated quote services spend specialize in options?

- If yes, will their program give me a chance to punch in trade parameters and screen for good trading chances?

- Does the brokerage firm's program have any comparable services to assist me with options analysis?

4. Timely executions and confirmations. The broker's order entry program ought to give guide access to the electronic trading frameworks of the suitable trades and,

once your trades qualify for programmed execution, report back a confirmation in few seconds — ideally to an area of the order-entry screen where you can quickly observe that you got your fill. In the event that the trade does not qualify the bill for programmed execution, it ought to show up in a corner on your screen intended to give you a chance to monitor your working orders.

5. The ability of the framework to deal with high-volume circumstances. The broker's database ought to have the adequate reserve processing capacity to deal with additional overwhelming order streams — and the firm ought to have a framework set up to manage quick economic situations as successfully as possible. (No firm is flawless when such circumstances occur, yet they ought to try to at the very least — not simply hurl their hands and say, "Sorry" or "Too bad!")

6. Commission costs. Numerous traders would put commissions much higher on the list than No. 6; however, our reasoning is unique. To mind: What great are low commissions in the event that you get lousy prices, moderate executions, and terrible (or no) benefits? Ensure the broker gives you all that you need — and require — and do not stress on the chance that it cost a couple of additional dollars. You will likely influence it up on your trades, at any rate. Do, in any case, demand that the broker's fees, at any rate, be competitive; you need to pay for what you get — not pay to get gouged. Additionally, make sure to get some information about possibly precarious things covered up underneath a guarantee of low commissions — e.g; a commission rate of $1 per option will not help you a whole lot if the firm forces a $50 least on each order.

7. Customer support. Very important! It is a must-have — ideally by telephone, not only online, by email, or through a self-improvement menu on the site (in spite of the fact that it is pleasant to have those choices too). Likewise, see if support is accessible simply amid business hours — or terribly, just when the market's open. Your goal is to guarantee that the help services will be accessible on the occasions you really require help.

8. Backups for order execution in case of technical issues. As we will talk about in one moment, there will be times when things turn out badly — even with the best broker and the most superb programming. In the event that it occurs within trading hours, your broker must have a backup framework to manage it. That implies having enough telephone lines and in-house individuals to deal with

OPTIONS TRADING STRATEGIES

client calls and the sudden flood of disconnected order stream. All things considered, no trader who frantically needs to escape a position 30 minutes before the end wants to call his broker and hear a tinny, computer voice: "All agents are presently occupied; however, your call is vital to us. Please stay on the line; a delegate will be with you in roughly 45 minutes" — soon after you've lost your shirt!

9. Simple access to account data. Trading capability is not the sole key to accomplishment in options trading — money management is similarly vital. But it is difficult to deal with your money in the event that you cannot easily access the status of your account. With a decent broker software program, you ought to have the capacity to get to all key data — including open positions and their values, balances, total equity, available equity, result of recent trades, and profit/loss statements (ideally, the ones you can ask for by period or on a year-to-date premise). The perfect framework will likewise play out the majority of the math and the greater part of the accounting capacities for you.

10. Security of individual and financial data. Numerous individuals fear to do anything online in light of the fact that they fear a hacker or another person will discover excessively about them, take their personalities — or, surprisingly more terrible, take their money. Insubstantial part, these fears are unreasonable — particularly inside the frameworks of America's financial services systems, which were planned in view of security and had unique assurances, set up. Therefore, most brokerage frameworks are as secure as it is presently conceivable to make them. All things considered; it never hurts to make an inquiry.

Minimum Equity Requirement

The United States Securities and Exchange Commission (SEC) and the Financial Industry Regulatory Authority (FINRA) enforce rules on people who day trade. They use the term Pattern Day Trader to qualify those who can engage in day trading with stock brokerage firms operating in the United States.

The qualified pattern day traders as those who day trades, i.e.; takes and closes positions within the same day, at least four times in the last five business days. The SEC and FINRA require that pattern day traders must have a minimum equity balance of $25,000 in their brokerage account before they day trade. When the equity balance falls below this amount for one reason or another, brokers are compelled to prohibit pattern day traders from executing new day trades until they're able to bring their equity back up to at least $25,000.

Many newbie day traders, especially those who only have this minimum amount, look at this rule as more of a hindrance to day trading glory rather than a protective fence against day trading tragedies. They don't realize that it's meant to keep them from taking excessive day trading risks that can easily wipe out their trading capitals in an instant because of their brokers' commissions and fees.

While this rule is the minimum requirement under the law, many brokers and dealers may use a stricter definition of a pattern day trader for purposes of transacting with them. The best thing to do is to clarify this minimum equity requirement with your chosen broker to avoid confusion later on.

If you can't afford the $25,000 minimum equity requirement for day trading, you can opt to trade with an offshore broker instead. They're brokerage firms that operate outside the United States, such as Capital Markets Elite Group Limited, which operates out of Trinidad and Tobago. Because these brokers operate outside the jurisdiction of FINRA, they're not subject to the pattern day trader rule. This means you're also not subject to the same minimum amount.

But before you think of trading with offshore brokers, keep in mind that these brokers are beyond the juridical reach of the SEC and FINRA. This means if anything goes wrong, you can't count on the Federal Government to help you out. If you want to use them to avoid the pattern day trader rule, just make sure to limit the amount of day trading equity you'll place with such brokers to an amount that you're comfortable risking or losing.

Direct-Access and Conventional Brokers

Conventional brokers normally reroute their customers' orders, including yours, to other firms through some sort of pre-agreed upon order processing scheme. Thus, executing your orders through conventional brokers involve more steps and can take significantly more time. And when it comes to day trading, speed is essential.

Conventional brokers are often referred to as full-service brokers because they tend to provide customers with other services such as market research and investment advice, among others. Because of these "extras," their commissions and fees are usually much higher than direct-access brokers. Conventional or full-service brokers are ideal for long-term investors and swing traders because they're not as particular with the speed of trade executions as day traders are.

Compared to full-service or conventional brokers, direct-access brokers focus more on the speed of trade executions than research and advisory services. And because they often skip the extra services to focus on providing fast and easy access to the stock market, they charge fewer commissions and fees. This has earned many of them the alias "discount brokers."

Direct-access brokers use very powerful computer programs and provide customers with online platforms through which they can directly trade the stock market, whether it's the NASDAQ or the NYSE. And while they provide the necessary trade execution speeds required in day trading, they're not perfect, and they have their share of challenges.

One such challenge is the imposition of monthly trading volume quotas. If you fail to meet their minimum monthly trading volume, they'll charge you an "inactivity fee," which often serves as their minimum monthly commission from your and all their other clients' accounts. However, not all discount brokerage firms impose inactivity fees.

Another challenge particular to direct-access brokers concerns newbie day traders, i.e.; familiarity with direct-access trading. With conventional brokers, all a newbie trader needs to do is tell their broker the details of their orders, and the broker will be the one to take care of all things related to executing their orders in the market. With direct-access brokers, the day trader executes the orders through the broker's online platform or software.

This can be quite challenging for newbie day traders because apart from choosing their SIPs, they also need to know how to execute their orders on the platform properly. But since day trading is a more sophisticated form of stock market trading, the chances are high that newbie day traders have enough experience with direct-access trading already.

But just in case you're new to both direct-access brokerage trading and day trading, your best bet would be to practice on a broker's trading simulator before you even consider opening and trading a real account with that broker. That way, you'll have one less thing to think about when you finally start to day trade.

The Trading Platform

A trading platform pertains to the computer program or software that you'll use to day trade. This is different from the direct-access broker itself, but many traders make the mistake of thinking they're the same.

The trading platform is what you'll use to send your orders to the stock exchange, which the direct-access broker will clear on your behalf. While it's different from the direct-access brokers, it's not unusual for such brokers to develop and have their clients use their proprietary trading platforms to trade stocks in the exchange.

The number and quality of the features of trading platforms influence the price direct-access brokers charge their clients for their services. The more features a platform has, the higher the commissions and fees may be and vice versa.

A very important feature that you should look for in a trading platform is Hotkeys. Without them, you may not be able to execute trades fast enough to make them profitable. Considering that day trading focuses on stocks with relatively high volatility, being a second or two late can spell the difference between taking and closing positions at the ideal prices and missing out on profitable day trading opportunities.

Brokers have a greater margin for profit in option trades, so the competition between these platforms is quite high. But here are some of the platforms that stand out –

<u>TD Ameritrade</u>

This platform has been the first choice for traders for quite a long time and for a good reason. There is no base commission involved in the case of options trades. If someone is performing online trades that are self-directed, then it costs $0.65 for every contract. Another thing to note is that they do not have a system of minimum balance; however, if you want to get access to certain privileges in the advanced section or if you want to do margin trading, then an amount of $2000 has to be maintained in your account. If you have been trading actively on their platform, only then will you get access to the assets that are not so popular, like the foreign exchanges and futures. In order to learn different strategies and get the hang of what options trading is, TD Ameritrade gives beginner traders access to different platforms.

Both multi-condition and simple orders are supported in the web-based platform of TD Ameritrade. But the thinkorswim platform of TD Ameritrade truly makes it stand out, and this can be used by experienced traders. This is also a paid platform where the user can get access to features like trigger orders, options statistics, and so on. However, you should note that an announcement was made in 2019, where TD Ameritrade was supposed to be acquired by Charles Schwab; however, the acquisition hasn't been completed yet.

The real-time data offered in the thinkorswim platform is quite advanced, and no matter how experienced or picky you are as a trader, this platform is definitely going to satisfy you. The impressive range of tools available on this platform will not only give you several historical info but also help you chart social sentiments or even practice trading with fake money. You are also going to get access to a special earning analysis tool in the thinkorswim setup where you can start planning even before a company's earnings release. You will get access to data from analysts of Wall Street.

E*TRADE

This is also a web-based platform, and the reason behind its popularity is its user-friendly nature. Previously, for options traders, the cost was $6.95 + $0.75 for every contract, but now, after October 2019, it has reduced to $0 + $0.65 for every contract.

The charting tool of this platform is great, and the zooming and panning features are quite smooth. In fact, there are a total of 32 drawing tools and 119 optional technical indicators. The position management for options trading is seamless with features like real-time streaming Greeks, custom grouping, risk analysis, and so on. If you are a beginner, then you can reap the full benefits of the Snapshot Analysis Tool of E*TRADE, where you will be taught how to start trading in options.

The research findings provided to the users by this platform is exceptional. If you are someone who depends on recommendations given by analysts, then you are going to get it here from multiple third parties, but you are not going to get the live broadcasting feature that is present in TD Ameritrade.

Another point worth noting is that the mobile trading feature of this platform is quite advanced. You are going to get a customized dashboard along with research ratings from third parties, and the app has been built for speed.

Charles Schwab

This is the best platform for every beginner, and you are literally going to feel at home here. If you are interested in knowing the ins and outs of options trading, this platform is where you need to be because of its extensive range of resources. Also, they are not going to charge you any base fee for the trades and only charge a fee of $0.65 for every contract and, thus, is the same as TD Ameritrade.

The more time you spend on trading, the more experienced you become, and so the platform will gradually grow its features for you. The investing platforms of Charles Schwab have various trading calculators and advanced charting tools that you are going to get access to with time.

The in-house research offered by Charles Schwab is nothing like you have ever seen. It is not only engaging but also refreshes constantly. The Street Smart Edge is the downloadable platform of Charles Schwab, and it has almost everything you need for options trading. Thus, you can call Charles Schwab and all-in-one package.

And as far as beginners are concerned, this platform is going to provide you with an unforgettable learning and educational experience. You are not only going to learn about options trading but any other investment topic you wish to learn about. But a drawback is that they do not have an option to track your learning progress, which is something you are going to get in TD Ameritrade.

Trade Station

Lastly, another trading platform that you should definitely check out for options trading is Trade Station because of the seamless experience they provide. As far as trader technology is concerned, this platform is considered to be a leader, and for a good reason. There are various commission structures available on their platform, and this is where most people get confused. But the two most common structures are the TS Go and TS Select. Here, you are not only going to get some free-market data, but they are also comparatively easy to understand.

In TS Select, you have to deposit a minimum amount of $2000, and with it, you will be given access to all the three platforms they have. For the options trades, for every contract, you will have to pay $0.60. In TS Go, there is no minimum amount required to be deposited, and for every contract in options trades, you have to pay $0.50. But there is also a limitation in TS Go — you will have access to all the platforms, but a $10 fee will be levied whenever you place trades on the Trade Station desktop.

On the other hand, the tools that you are going to get on this platform are quite diverse and rich in depth. They have access to historical data spanning 40 years, and options trading will seem easy with them. They offer advanced position analysis and custom grouping features.

Best Tools for Options Trading

When you are trading in the stock market, you obviously want to minimize your returns and, at the same time, maximize your profits, but for that, you also need to have some insight into the market. For this, the right tools can help you a lot, and here, in this section, I am going to provide you with a list of such tools that you can put to use.

Trade-Ideas

This is a standalone software that helps in scanning stocks. The analysis tools present in this software are quite impressive and does a lot of legwork for you. The market scanners are all strategy-based and will help you find some unique trading opportunities in real-time. You are also going to get access to several tutorials and videos that will help you learn about the system, and you will also get access to a chat room where you can discuss important matters with active traders.

Tradingview.com

Whether you are an experienced and advanced trader or just a basic one, tradingview.com has some of the best financial visualization and analytical tools available for you. You will be able to perform real-time analysis of different types of assets making options trading easier than ever before. In fact, if you want, you can customize your own signals with the help of the built-in indicators and also join the chat room to discuss trades with other active traders.

There is a feature of the social platform, which is really a boon because it enables you to share your experiences with others and also learn from others' experiences, thereby improving your skillset. The best thing is that if you want to test this website, you can get their basic package, which is absolutely free of cost, and then for a nominal fee, you can get access to the premium package. Also, all of these features are accessible at any time and from any device. If you don't want to miss out on anything, then you simply have to set the real-time alerts.

E*TRADE Mobile

As far as trading technology is concerned, E*TRADE Mobile is definitely one of the firsts. They also promise to provide you with some really advanced features through their app that you can access from your tablets and mobile phones. So, whether you are into options trading or you prefer to on-the-go trading, this app is exactly what you need in your life. There is another special feature in the app that is quite unique, and that is – they have a barcode scanner, yes, you have heard me right. If you find a product that you love and you want to know more about the company, then you simply have to scan the barcode.

The advanced platform is also going to provide you with educational material to upgrade your knowledge in the field of options trading. You can access performance-over-time charts and comparison charts and also build watch lists based on your criteria. These watch lists are totally customizable. There is an options roll tool in the app with the help of which the expiration date of your options can be extended. Moreover, everything that you do on the app is synced automatically to your desktop account so that you don't lose any information, and even if you log into a different device, you can simply pick up where you left off.

Scanz

They were previously known by the name of Equity Feed and they are basically a trading platform. They offer you real-time quotes, live news feeds, and live screening, and all of these services can be availed on a subscription basis. The scanning technology of this app is very powerful and does an in-depth scan of the market. You can also get a lot of help from their decision support, market monitoring, and alert management features.

Flow Algo

When it comes to options trading, Flow Algo is another very helpful tool for everyone. They are mainly focused on the stock and equity options markets, and they are a data algorithm tool. Different data points are considered in their analysis process, such as order type, order volume, the pattern of order filling, speed of the order, average volume, and so on. The tool has this incredible power of filtering what is most important for you and what is not and, thus, shows you only those things that are meaningful to you.

So, as you must have understood by now, investments in the options word are quite flexible, and having the right platform or tool by your side can make a lot of difference.

If you want to maintain a constant income stream from options, then taking the help of the right tools and platforms is of utmost importance. I hope that this guide has helped you gain some insight into this world, and please use it to make your selection of platforms and tools as you start your journey in options trading.

Real-Time Market Data

Unlike long-term investors and swing traders who only need end-of-day price data that are available for free online, day traders need real-time data as the trading day unfolds because they need to get in and out of positions within a matter of hours, minutes, or even seconds. And unfortunately, access to real-time intraday price data isn't free, and you'll need to pay monthly fees to your direct-access broker or the platform owner (if different from the brokerage firm) for them. Just ask your direct-access broker for details on their monthly fees for access to real-time day trading data.

Two of the most basic types of data that you'll need to look at as a day trader are the bid and ask prices. The bid prices are the prices at which other traders and investors are willing to buy a particular stock. The ask prices are the prices at which other traders and investors are willing to sell a particular stock.

The bid and ask prices are arranged such that the best price is at the top. The best bid price is the highest one, i.e.; the best price for sellers is the highest price at which buyers are willing to buy. The best ask price, on the other hand, is the lowest price at which sellers are willing to sell. It's considered the best price from the perspective of buyers. Bid and ask prices also indicate the number of shares that other traders and investors are willing to buy or sell at specific prices. The bid prices are usually listed on the left side while the ask prices are usually listed on the right such that the best bid and ask prices are right beside each other. If you want to execute your buy orders immediately, you "buy up" the best ask price. If you want to immediately execute your sell orders, "sell down" at the best bid price.

The Day Trading Orders

The three most important types of day trading orders are market, limit, and marketable limit orders.

Market orders refer to orders to buy or sell stocks at their current market prices for immediate execution. If you remember from earlier, these refer to buying up at the best current ask price or selling down at the best bid price.

Depending on market conditions and subsequent price movements during the day, market orders may be the worst or best prices to trade-in. For example, if you send a market order to sell when the bid-ask prices are $1.00-$1.05 and by the time your order hits the market, the bid-ask prices shift to $0.95-$1.01, your sell order will be done at $0.95. In this example, your sell proceeds get cut by a minimum of five cents multiplied by the number of shares you sold.

CHAPTER 6:

Which Technical Indicator Do I Often Use for Trading?

Specialized examination of protections depends on the rule that previous value developments in a budgetary instrument are an indicator of things to come in the cost. Trading volume (the quantity of protections being exchanged) is frequently joined with value development to help improve these value expectation models. The specialized investigation of stocks depends on the rule that previous value developments are an indicator of things to come moves in cost. Trading volume (the number of shares exchanged) is frequently joined with earlier value development to help improve these value forecast models. The essentials of developing a candle and a bar diagram. Graphs containing these figures are promptly accessible on the web. There are some essential candle designs that numerous specialized brokers watch for and base their exchanges on.

Candlestick basics: how a candle or bar outline is built and what it enlightens you concerning the opening and shutting cost during a period just as the highs and lows of that period.

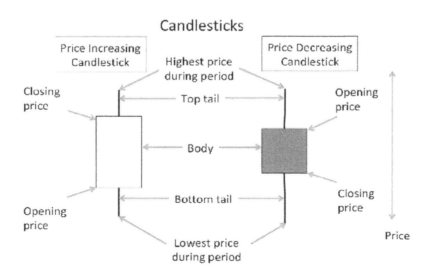

Step by step instructions to develop or distinguish a bullish candle (cost moving higher) and a bearish candle (price moving lower). A few inversion candles were examined, including the accompanying:

- **Immersing flame:** one huge light that is completely inundated and moves the other way of the past fire. This illustration shows examples of a gap up and a gap down between trading sessions.

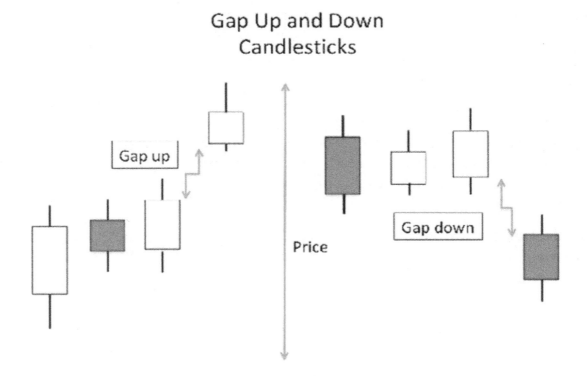

- **Haram cross candle** resembles a cross with a next to nobody and frequently roughly equivalent top and base tails. This chart of TZA shows an engulfing candle associated with a change in trend. In addition, the chart shows a haram cross, which also indicates a potential change in stock price direction.

- **Gravestone Doji**: shows that the cost of the stock opened low, it rose in price, however then dropped back and shut genuinely close to the open value, its long upper tail demonstrates conceivable bearish activity.

- **Dragonfly Doji:** shows that the cost of the stock opened high, it dropped in price, however then expanded and shut genuinely close to the open value, and its long lower tail demonstrates conceivable bullish activity.

Inundating candles and Doji can show a pattern inversion. You can exchange these as a pattern inversion and particularly with other affirming markers like the MACD and RSI. You can likewise hope to check whether there has been some principal move that has made the stock or segment switch.

This chart of PFE shows both gravestone and dragonfly Doji candlesticks with corresponding stock price reversal action

- **Gaps** can be exchanged as a continuation exchange (the upswing or downtrend proceeds for an all-inclusive timeframe) or looked for an eruption. You can search for fixing or bottoming design because of overcompensation in value activity (which demonstrates that the purchasers or vendors are depleted and that an inversion in cost is going to occur) and afterward take an inversion exchange. A chart of WMT shows the gap in price from a close one day to the open on trading day

OPTIONS TRADING STRATEGIES

Gapping value activity typically happens between trading meetings. The size of the hole is frequently petite; however, on different occasions, it tends to be enormous. Bigger apertures are typically brought about by some new data that has become exposed, which influences the assessment of the brokers and financial specialists toward the stock. It could be negative news, for example, a medication test disappointment or it could be uplifting news, for example, the declaration of another item dispatch. After a hole has happened, 1 of 3 things will occur:

- gap and go

- gap and solidify

- Gap and pullback (called "filling the hole")

For a swing trader, gaps can be hard to exchange after they have just occurred. Gaps can bring about overcompensating to some news and those eruptions can be the most recent daily or they can keep going for a few days. In an improving business sector, a swing trader can take a situation during the first day of the gap up. They could take a location close to the furthest limit of the day if the stock keeps on inclining higher and finishes off the day near or at the high. There is a decent possibility under this situation (a stable market and a substantial stock value activity) that the cost will gap up again on the next day.

Another approach to playing by gaps is to utilize the gap and fill standard. Regularly the focuses where a stock gapped higher or lower become, individually, levels of opposition or backing. Eruptions in the market happen always, and in the end, these overcompensating will address themselves. A swing broker can look for top or base examples in stock that would demonstrate the purchasers or vendors are depleted and that an inversion in cost is going to occur (which will speak to a trading opportunity).

CHAPTER 7:

What Kind of Trading Strategy Are Short Selling and Margin Trading?

Short Selling

Many traders use the concept of short selling when they invest in the market. Short selling refers to when you need to borrow stock from the holder and sell that stock to another buyer. You will then wait for the price of the stock to fall before you give the stocks back to the lender. This is one of the easiest ways in which you can capitalize on the volatility of the prices. Having said that, you must make the right decisions about the investments you make and not invest or borrow useless stocks. You must always ensure that you maintain a wide margin that will allow you to make a few mistakes. You should ensure that you have enough capital to support any other investments if things never work out. It is always a good idea to buy shares back at the earliest if you believe that the price of the stocks will continue to increase.

Understanding Margin Trading

Brokerage firms and financial institutions that allow day trading on their platforms provide margin facilities to their clients to trade stocks or other financial assets at a fraction of the original cost. This called margin trading, and it is usually restricted to intraday trade.

With the margin facility, a trader with $ 20 can trade a stock that costs $ 200. Margin trading involves borrowing funds from the brokerage firm and trading that borrowed money many times over.

Margin trading allows day traders to trade multiple times in a session with a small investing capital. For prudent day traders, it is a good facility that they use for their profits. But for beginners, it may turn into a trap, making them greedy and losing money by over-trading. Margin facility gives a false sense to day traders of having more money than they have. During trading, they forget that they're trading on borrowed money and sometimes accumulate more losses. Also, the brokerage charges pile up, and total losses for them become higher than the money in the account. In such situations, traders get a call from their brokerage, demanding to deposit money in their accounts to cover the deficit. This is known as the margin call and is a signal that the trader is accumulated losses.

Like nuclear power, margin trading can be good in experienced hands and destructive in the hands of novice traders who become greedy for its power.

Therefore, margin trading should be done in a calculated way. Traders should keep an account of how many trades they have done in a single session and how much loss or profits they have made.

A margin facility is good for those traders who have strict rules for money management and control over their trading habits. By trading carefully, they can increase their profits with just a small investment. Trading on margin increases a trader's trading power because, with the help of margin, they can trade for a greater amount than the money in their trading accounts will allow. If your brokerage firm offers a merging facility for day trading, consider and plan carefully how you will use it before making any decision.

In margin trading, all open positions are squared off before markets close for that session, and traders are not allowed to carry forward positions that have been opened using the margin facility.

Money & Risk Management Techniques

For successful trading in the stock markets, money management and risk management are crucial steps. Stock markets can turn highly volatile at times, and if you are not careful about protecting your money and the risk of open trades, you can suffer huge monetary losses.

Therefore, the first step in day trading should be: learn how to reduce trading risk and manage your capital investment so you can tolerate the normal losses in day trading. Money management is like strengthening your defenses so you can survive in the stock market to trade another day. Safe trading practices to protect your money can increase your profits. A lack of it can also double your losses. Money and risk management can be the difference between the success and failure of a day trader. Often, beginners are so focused on making profits in stock markets, they forget to protect their invested capital, and soon, and their losses wipe out the whole trading capital.

OPTIONS TRADING STRATEGIES

"A penny saved is a penny earned" perfectly explains the money management principle in stock trading. Often, day traders stay in a loss-making trade, thinking soon the losses will stop, and the trend will reverse to award those profits. This is the biggest mistake they can make. It is always safer to exit a loss-making trade with a small loss and protect your capital from being wiped out completely. Putting a stop loss in all your trades is the safest way of protecting your trading capital.

Part of good money management is using just a fraction of your trading capital on one trade. In other words, never put all your money on a single trade. As they say, 90% of traders do not make profits in day trading. A big reason for this failure is not paying attention to money management. If you keep on betting on stock prices for rising or falling with no proper strategy and risk management, then it is pure gambling and not any intelligent business venture.

Take day trading as a business, do it with proper money management, learn how you can reduce the risk in your trades; you will reduce the number of potential losses, and increase potential profits. Keep your trading cost to a minimum. Before opening any trade, always decide how much loss you will allow for that trade and put a stop loss to cover that much amount. Markets will come back the next day, but you should be left with enough capital to trade when markets open for the next session.

Risk Management Techniques

In day trading, there is always a risk that you will lose money. Now, if you want to start day trading as a career, learn a few techniques that will reduce and manage the risk of potential losses. By taking steps to manage the risk, you reduce the potential day trading losses.

To stay in the day trading business for the long term, you must protect your trading capital. By reducing the risk of losses, you open the possibilities of future profits and a sustainable day trading business.

If you plan well, prepare your trading strategies before starting to trade; you increase the possibility of a stable trading practice, which can lead to profits. Therefore, it is essential to prepare your trading plans every day, create trading strategies, and follow your trading rules. These three things can make or break your day trading business. Professional day traders always plan their trades first and then trade their plans. This can be understood by an example of two imaginary traders. Suppose there are two traders, trading in the same stock market, trading the same stock. One of them has prepared his trading plan and knows when and how he will trade. The other trader has done no planning and is just sitting there, taking the on-the-spot decisions for buying or selling the stock. Who do you think will be more successful? The one who is well prepared, or the one who has no inkling of what he will do the next second?

The second risk management technique is using stop orders. Use these orders to decide to fix your stop -loss and profit booking points, which will take emotions out of your decision-making process, and automatically cut the losses or book the profit for you.

Many a time, profitable trade turns into loss-making because markets change their trend, but traders do not exit their positions, hoping to increase profits. Therefore, it is necessary to keep a profit booking point and exit the profitable trades at that point. Keeping a fixed profit booking point can also help you calculate your returns with every trade and help you avoid taking the unnecessary risk for further trades.

Taking emotions out of day trading is a very important requirement for profitable trading. Do not prejudge the trend in stock markets, which many day traders do and trade against markets, ending with losses.

CHAPTER 8:

How Hard Can the Trading Possibly Be?

Options trading is not something that is for everyone.

You Are Able to Weather the Storm

Options prices can move a lot over the course of short time periods. So, someone who likes to see their money protected and not losing any is not going to be suitable for options trading. Now, we all want to come out ahead, so I am not saying that you have to be happy about losing money in order to be an options trader. What you have to be willing to do is calmly observe your options losing money, and then be ready to stick it out in order to see gains return in the future. This is akin to riding a real roller coaster, but it is a financial roller coaster. Options do not slowly appreciate the way a Warren Buffett investor would hope to see.

Options move big on a percentage basis, and they move fast. If you are trading multiple contracts at once, you might see yourself losing $500 and then earning $500 over a matter of a few hours. In this sense, although most options traders are not "day traders" technically speaking, you will be better off if you have a little bit of a day trading mindset.

You Don't Make Emotional Decisions

Since options are, by their nature, volatile, and very volatile for many stocks, coming to options trading and being really emotional about it is not a good way to approach your trading. If you are emotional, you are going to exit your trades at the wrong time in 75% of cases.

You don't want to make any sudden moves when it comes to trading options. As we have said, you should have a trading plan with rules on exiting your positions, stick to those rules and you should be fine.

Be a Little Bit Math-Oriented

In order to really understand options trading and be successful, you cannot be shy about numbers. Options trading is a numbers game. That doesn't mean you have to drive over to the nearest university and get a statistics degree. But if you do understand probability and statistics, you are going to be a better options trader. Frankly, it's hard to see how you can be a good options trader without having a mind for numbers. Some math is at the core of options trading and you cannot get around it.

You Are Market-Focused

You don't have to set up a day trading office with ten computer screens so you can be tracking everything by the moment, but if you are hoping to set up a trade and lazily come back to check it three days later, that isn't going to work with options trading. You do need to be checking your trades a few times a day. You also need to be keeping up with the latest financial and economic news, and you need to keep up with any news directly related to the companies you invest in or any news that could impact those companies. If the news does come out, you are going to need to make decisions if it's news that isn't going to be favorable to your positions. Also, you need to be checking the charts periodically, so you have an idea of where things are heading for now.

Focus on a Trading Style

As you can see, there are many different ways that you can trade options. In my opinion, sticking to one or two strategies is the best way to approach options trading. I started off buying call options, but now, I focus on selling put credit spreads and iron condors. You should pick what you like best and also something that aligns with your goals. I moved into selling put credit spreads and iron condors because I became interested in the idea of making a living from options trading with regular income payments, rather than continuing to buy calls and hope that the share price would go up. There is no right or wrong answer, pick the trading style that is best suited to your own personal style and needs.

Keep Detailed Trading Journals

It's easy to fool yourself when trading options, especially if you are a beginner. I hate to make the analogy, but this is kind of like going to the casino. If you have friends that gamble at casinos, then you are going to notice that they tend to remember the wins, and they will forget all the times that they gambled and lost. I had a cousin that won a boat, and she was always bragging about how she won a boat at the casino. I remember telling her that yes she won a boat, but she paid $65,000 more than the boat was worth to the casino over the years. You don't want to get in the same situation with your options trading. It can be an emotional experience because trading options are active and fast-paced. When you have a profitable trade, it will be exciting. But you need to keep a journal to record all of your trades, in order to know exactly what the real situation is. That doesn't mean you quit if you look at your journal and find out you have a losing record, what you do is figure out why your trades aren't profitable and then make adjustments.

Options Traders Are Flexible

I have said this before, but one thing you need to remember about options trading is you can make money no matter what happens to the stock. So, you need to avoid falling into the trap of only trading options to make money one way. Most frequently, people do what they have been brainwashed to do and they will trade call options hoping to profit from rising share prices. If you are in that mindset now, you need to challenge yourself and begin trading in different ways, so you can actually experience making money from declining stock prices, or in the case of iron condors, stock prices that don't even change at all. You need to be able to adapt to changing market conditions in order to profit as an options trader. So, don't entrap yourself by only using one method. Earlier, I said to use one or two styles, but you should be ready to branch out when market conditions change. Remember this – market conditions always change eventually. As I am writing, we are in the midst of a long-term bull market, but it won't last forever.

Take a Disciplined Approach

Don't just buy options for a certain stock because it feels good. You need to do research on your stocks. That will include doing fundamental analysis. This is going to mean paying attention to the history of a stock, knowing what the typical ranges are for, stock in recent history is, and also reading through the company's financial statements and prospectus. Remember, I suggest picking three companies to trade options on for a year and also two index funds.

The index funds require less research, but for the three companies that you pick, you should get to know those companies inside and out. Stick with them for a year, at the end of each year, evaluate each company. Then decide if you want to keep them and bring them forward into the following year's trades. If one company is not working out for you, then move on and try a different company.

CHAPTER 9:

What Are the Most Popular Options Trading Strategies Used by Hedge Fund Managers?

Covered Calls

The covered call option strategy requires you to write a call option for the stock that you purchase outright or already own. With covered calls, you earn a premium when you sell and you also get all the benefits that come with owning the asset up to its strike price, where it will be called away.

There are various ways to implement the covered call option strategy and a lot of investors use them differently. You can use the strategy to gain more profit from the position of the stock if the market trading is relatively flat. This is a great option since aside from the premium, you also get capital gains if there's an increase in the value of the underlying stock. 'Out of the money' calls trades are often made when the market outlook is neutral or bullish.

The covered call option strategy is typically opened by 30 – 60 days before it expires. This benefits you due to the time decay factor. Of course, your goals dictate the optimum time to implement this strategy. For example, if you want to sell calls while making money with the stock, it works better if the difference between the price of the stock and its strike price is not so big. If you want to sell both the call and the stock, the price of the stock should stay above its strike price until the contract expires.

Buying and Selling Puts

Generally speaking, this is a better option for beginning traders. Our belief is that starting out selling covered call options, then moving on to limited purchases of call options is the best way to get started in options trading. Once you gain experience in that, you can move on to trading options themselves and also with buying and selling put options.

Truthfully, puts aren't really all that different than calls, because a call is based on an educated hunch that some stock is going to go up in price in the coming weeks or months. A put is a bet that the opposite will occur, in other words, that the stock market price is going to decrease in the coming weeks or months.

ITM

ITM options are options that have an intrinsic value. In other words, if they were to be exercised at that point, they would yield some money. Any call option with a strike price less than the market price of the underlying stock/index is an ITM option. Any put option that has a strike-price greater than the market price of the underlying stock/index is an ITM option. The intrinsic value of an ITM option is the positive difference between its underlying stock's market price and the option's strike price.

OTM

OTM options are the opposite of ITM options. They do not have any intrinsic value. At the time of expiry, every single OTM option expires worthless. Any call option with its strike-price greater than the market price of its underlying stock/index and any put option with its strike-price less than the market price of its underlying stock/index is OTM options.

Iron Condor

This one is considered a credit spread. You will still get the advantage against the time decay issue, but it is considered a non-directional strategy because you are betting against both directions rather than just one. You would choose to work with this strategy when you have a stock that is either stable or not moving all that much, or you have one that goes up and down, but those movements stay within a specified range and you think the stock will stay there for the short term. The risk of the iron condor strategy is considered low.

Iron Butterfly

An iron butterfly is a different type of trade that also involves four options. This time, you are hoping to hit a specific share price to maximize profits, but the trade can also be set up with a directional bias one way or the other. In the case of an iron butterfly, we modify the iron condor by selling put and call options at the same strike price.

Collar Strategy

A collar is a useful strategy to use if you already own long position shares of an underlying stock that has a proven record of substantial gains that makes it worth betting on again in the future. Putting a collar in place then allow you to maximize your gains across all angles. Creating a collar is as easy as generating a put that is already out of the money while at the same time writing a call that is also out of the money and is related to the same underlying stock. This strategy is useful if you want to protect yourself from a specific loss, as the put will keep most of your profit in place should the underlying stock sour. You then fund this level of protection with the second call, ensuring you have the profit to pay for the protection. You may also find this strategy helpful if you need to mitigate excess costs by allowing the collar to roll over indefinitely.

Short Put

A short put option practice means you are wagering that the price of a stock will go up or stay as is until the contract expires. If the put expires as 'out of the money', or more than the strike price, you get to keep the entire premium.

As the short put seller, you are forced to buy the stock at its strike price if your buyer chooses to exercise the option.

A short put can be a very useful strategy since it gives you increased income by receiving premiums from other investors who wagered that the price of the stock will fall. Hence, if you use the short put strategy, you get the premium and also protect yourself when the market is flat or there is very little movement. Then again, you need to sell your puts sparingly since you are obligated to buy the shares if the stock goes lower than strike-price when the contract expires.

Short puts can be used to get better purchasing prices on stocks that are overpriced by selling these puts at strike prices that are much lower, where you would choose to purchase the stock.

Long Put

This is when you buy a put in anticipation of the price falling.

Credit Spread

An option spread is another way for new traders to participate with lower risk. Unfortunately, that also means a lower reward. These trades involve buying or selling two options, one at the money and one further out of the money option. For example, say 'Proctor and Gamble' is currently at a market price of 82. An investor who owns several hundred shares of PG, structures a Bear Call Spread by selling a call on PG with a strike price of 77 for $4.75 and at the same time, buys a call at a strike price of 84 for $0.10. In this contract, he collects the difference of $4.65. As long as the market stays between 77 and 84. If it stays within that range, both options will expire, and he keeps the money. If PG moves above 84, he can buy the stock at 84. If PG falls below 77, which is unlikely, the option will expire.

Bull Put Spreads consist of selling a put with a strike price above the current market and buying a put at an out of the money level below the current market. The gain for the investor is the difference between the two premiums, not a lot of money but low risk.

Debit Spread

Unlike a credit spread where the seller receives cash into his or her account, debit spreads instead carry an upfront cost. The premium is paid from the investor's account when the position is opened, and this is referred to as a debit. This type of strategy is mostly used to offset the costs associated with having long option positions. This results because the premium received from long components is more than the premium received from short components. As a result of this, the net debit is the highest possible value for loss in this type of options strategy. Losses are thus limited.

Strangles and Straddles

This is a debit spread that is also non-directional, just like the iron condor. It does have the disadvantage of not being able to work against the time decay issue. You would choose this strategy any time that the market, or at least the stock you are working with, is going to be really volatile for a short amount of time. It is used by traders who see a high probability of imminent sharp rise and fall in the stock price. This method can be used to catch both of them if you are not sure which way the market will go. The risk on this one is pretty high; if the market doesn't get as volatile as you predicted, you could lose a lot of money. However, there is the potential for unlimited profits, so if there is going to be a big change in the market soon, this may be the right one to go with.

Remember that when you are picking out the strategy that you want to use, the directional debit strategies are going to help you to get a fast and bigger return. They have a good risk to reward ratio, and they have the issue of time decay that is working with them. This is why most professional traders stay away from the debit spreads in most cases, even though these may look like good options to work with.

If you are looking for the strategy that is going to be the most consistent when it comes to generating income, you will want to work with the Iron Condor. This is because, in addition to getting the same benefits as the other credit spreads when it comes to time decay and probability, it is also considered a neutral position. The stock can go up and down with this strategy, and you still have the potential to make a profit, as long as your strike points are in the right place.

Rolling Out Options

Rolling a trade simply means that you are simultaneously closing out your existing positions and opening new ones based on the same underlying stock. When rolling a position, you can change the strike price, the duration of the contract, or both. You can roll forward, which means to extend the expiration date for the option.

A roll-up means that you increase the strike price when you open the new contract. A roll-up is used on a call option when you believe the underlying stock is going to increase in price. When you are trading put options, you use a roll down. In that case, you close your option and reopen it with the same underlying stock but with a lower strike price. A higher strike price means that the new position will be cheaper. When rolling, you're going out in time for the deadline. When rolling a call, you're hoping that the stock will rise in price. In this case, you're rolling to an out of the money position. The price of the new call will drop. With a put, the opposite occurs, and the price of the new put will increase.

Options Greeks

The Greeks are a bunch of Greek letters, each of which symbolizes a different measurement of the option's volatility and behavior. The delta is the rate at which the price of the option changes with every unit change in the price of the underlying. For obvious reasons, options with a high delta are desirable although they are likely to go pear-shaped sooner as well.

CHAPTER 10:

How Many Years Does It Take to Master Options Trading?

Avoiding Common Pitfalls in Options Trading

It is completely understandable that a person without prior knowledge of how options trading works will make mistakes. It is, therefore, useful to present the most commonly made mistakes so that you can avoid them.

Optional trading is not easy. This is a proven fact and there is no argument about it. Every year several people fail and lose money in options trading. This article is for those who want to prosper in options trading.

To be honest, beginners can never be considered professionals by any stretch. Most of the beginner options traders even do not come from a finance background. As a result, they fail to understand the economy or the stock market and hence cannot cope with things happening the way they do.

In order to proceed with the trading of options, one should first realize that options trading is not the industry where he or she could become rich quickly. Understanding this in the first place will save thousands or maybe even millions. He or she needs to have a strong trading mentality which is something that can be learned over time. Here are some of the beginner's mistakes that should be avoided:

Not Creating a Non-Emotional Trading Plan

Mixing business with emotion is the worst mistake one could have ever done. Most of the beginners fail because of this. They should always follow proper business plans with objectives to achieve and rules and regulations to abide by. In order to become successful overnight, they often miss out on these principles and hence such an outcome. Human beings are emotional and eventually, they show that while making decisions. Thus, the rules, so that one could follow his or her own rules.

Letting Your Losses Build

In order to be truly successful, it is important to make a concentrated effort to keep your expectations for a trade and the reality of the trade separate. The fact of the matter is that once a trade enters losing territory it is unlikely to rebound enough that it actually makes a decent profit and as such, they find that it is best to nip losses in the bud as early as possible. New traders often make the mistake of sticking with certain trades, even after signs begin pointing to a loss because they take trading personally, possibly because they think a failed trade is a reflection on them, or because they simply don't like to lose. Regardless of the reasons behind it, doubling down on a losing trade is only ever asking for trouble.

Averaging Down

Most traders tend to wander across averaging down. It isn't what they had in mind when they first start to trade but end up doing so anyway. Several problems can arise when averaging down. The main thing is that they can lose a position that they are holding on to. This is sacrificing money and time. This money and time could be placed elsewhere that could prove itself to be better.

Not Having a Coach

Having a coach adds immense value to trading strategies. One aiming to become successful should have their own coach just like every sportsperson has their own coach. He or she may be good in their own way and might as well doing good in the trading field. However, to avoid silly and pointless mistakes while trading and to advance further and faster while earning higher returns, he or she certainly needs the advice of a coach.

Not Understanding Risks and Rewards

The underlying concept of risk and reward is not understood by most people. Often traders who have faced losses in their career at an early stage develop a fear of risks. Hence, they start making smaller deals to avoid any risk but end up earning less profit. Thus, they often get missed out on the rewards that are closely tied to the risks. Thus, with the right knowledge of reward and risk, one could avoid downfall in their business and earn huge profits.

Beginning with Buying OTM Call Options

OTM means out-of-money and refers to call options that have expired and have not produced a return. Many people consider these as a relatively safe investment, while actually, it is one of the hardest methods to make a profit. It also is a way that will not teach you anything while it will cost you money.

Doing Poor Allocation

Never commit more than 5% of your portfolio to one options trade. In as much as options have leverage and high earning potential, you cannot ignore the high level of risk exposure. Thus, you have to allocate prudently.

Not Having an Exit Plan

Before you start trading, you should fully understand what you're trying to get into. How much money do you intend to make? What are your risk-reduction measures? Once you have answered the critical questions, you will be in a position to make appropriate strategies and learn how to exit with the least possible scars when you're losing money.

Choosing an Inappropriate Date of Expiration

The date of expiration affects the price of an option. But due to incompetence and carelessness, many traders select dates of expiration that hurt their chances of making profits.

Buying an Option with High Volatility.

Another mistake that you can make is to purchase options in a time of high volatility. During these times, option premiums will often get overpriced, and if you purchase an option, you could still lose.

Using Brokers Who Charge Too Much

When you are investing, it is important to cut down your costs as much as possible. While you do not want to be cheap and cut corners, there are some brokers who will charge way more for their services compared to others. You can choose to go with another option that will save you some money.

You do need to do some research ahead of time. Just because a broker charges less doesn't mean that they are the best ones for you. There are many brokers who will charge you a fair rate, but make sure that you look at some of the features that each one offers and pick one that will provide you with the results that you would like.

Doubling Risk to Cover Loss

Taking this strategy is very similar to a gambler entering a poker game with an all-or-nothing mindset after having just lost everything in his wallet. Strategies can either gain or lose capital and investors need to be sure they are not trying to overcompensate for the loss by investing in a bad trade. If a particular strategy is not working, the investor would be best off abandoning it altogether as soon as he or she is able, using the investor's personalized exit strategy.

Greed

Though it's exciting to be on the uptrend and reaping monetary rewards through options trading, it's paramount for investors to realize when they need to step back. This is where having an exit strategy on the uptrend comes in because eventually, the market will reverse itself and investors do not want to be caught losing all of their hard-earned money on the downswing just because they got a little greedy. This can be partially offset by constantly examining the time frame charts and searching for trade signals. When doing so, investors should not only look for new opportunities but also become aware of potential fiscally harmful situations.

Ignoring Future Trends

A common mistake among new investors is to confuse historical trends with future ones. Past trends are only indicative of future trends in that their shapes can be used to predict a change in the trend, which is what the pennant, flag, rectangle, triangle, wedge, and head-and-shoulders signals are used for. Confusing the two will lead investors to make inaccurate predictions and thus lose money on faulty strategies. Instead, investors should practice spotting future opportunities by examining old time frame charts, which will sharpen their skills and gain them future earnings.

Overtrading

The fact that in the options market you can control a much larger amount of stock with the same money than you can in the stock market is a huge advantage. But it can also turn into a big disadvantage if you're not careful about this. Yes, you can make bigger gains with a much smaller amount of money, and overtrading seems very tempting. But it might give you a false sense of wealth, making you feel like you're worth much more than you are. This further results in you trading an even higher number of options. It's a vicious cycle, and you should avoid overtrading actively.

NATHAN PRICE

CHAPTER 11:

How Can I Get Any Breaking News Earlier?

Identify the Fastest and Most Effective Strategy

Iron Butterfly

The last choice methodology we will show is the iron butterfly. In this procedure, a financial specialist will sell an at-the-cash put and purchase an out-of-the-cash put, while likewise selling an at-the-cash get and purchasing an out-of-the-cash call. All alternatives have a similar termination date and are on the equivalent fundamental resource. Albeit like a butterfly spread, this system varies in light of the fact that it utilizes the two calls and puts, instead of either.

This technique basically consolidates selling an at-the-cash straddle and purchasing defensive "wings." You can likewise think about the development as two spreads. It is entirely expected to have a similar width for the two spreads. The long out-of-the-cash call ensures against boundless drawbacks. The long out-of-the-cash put shields against drawback from the short put strike to zero. Benefit and misfortune are both restricted inside a particular range, contingent upon the strike costs of the alternatives utilized. Speculators like this technique for the salary it creates and the higher likelihood of a little increase with a non-unstable stock.

Iron Corridor

All alternatives have a similar lapse date and are on the equivalent hidden resource. Ordinarily, the put and call sides have a similar spread width. This exchanging system procures a net premium on the structure and is intended to exploit a stock encountering low unpredictability. Numerous merchants like this exchange for its apparent high likelihood of acquiring a limited quantity of premium.

In the P&L chart, the greatest increase is made when the stock stays in a generally wide exchanging extent, which would bring about the financial specialist gaining the all-out net credit got when building the exchange. The further away the stock travels through the short strikes (lower for the put, higher for the call), the more noteworthy the misfortune, up to the most extreme misfortune. Most extreme misfortune is generally essentially higher than the greatest increase, which instinctively bodes well, given that there is a higher likelihood of the structure completing with a little.

Long Call Butterfly Spread

The majority of the methodologies as yet have required a blend of two unique positions or agreements. In a long butterfly spread utilizing call choices, a speculator will join both a bull spread system and a bear spread procedure and utilize three diverse strike costs. All choices are for the equivalent fundamental resource and termination date.

For instance, a long butterfly spread can be built by acquiring one in-the-cash call alternative at a lower strike cost, while selling two at-the-cash call choices and getting one out-of-the-cash call choice. A reasonable butterfly spread will have a similar wing width. This model is known as a "call fly" and results in a net charge. A speculator would go into a long butterfly call spread when they think the stock won't move much by lapse.

In the P&L chart, the most extreme addition is made when the stock stays unaltered up until lapse (directly at the ATM strike). The further away the stock moves from the ATM strikes, the more prominent the negative change in P&L. Most extreme misfortune happens when the stock settles at the lower strike or underneath, or if the stock settles at or over the higher strike call. This procedure has both restricted upsides and constrained drawbacks.

Long Strangle

In a long choke choices technique, the financial specialist buys an out-of-the-cash get choice and an out-of-the-cash put choice at the same time on the equivalent hidden resource and lapse date. A financial specialist who uses this procedure accepts the basic resource's cost will encounter an enormous development yet is uncertain of which course the move will take. This could, for instance, be a bet on a profit discharge for an organization or an FDA occasion for a medicinal services stock. Misfortunes are restricted to the expenses (or premium spent) for the two alternatives. Chokes will quite often be more affordable than straddles on the grounds that the alternatives bought are out of the cash.

In the P&L chart, there are two breakeven focuses. This system winds up beneficial when the stock makes an extremely enormous move one way or the other. Once more, the speculator couldn't care less which bearing the stock moves, just that it is a more noteworthy move than the all-out premium the financial specialist paid for the structure.

Long Straddle

This technique ends up beneficial when the stock makes a huge move one way or the other. The financial specialist couldn't care less which course the stock moves just that it is a more noteworthy move than the all-out premium the speculator paid for the structure.

Defensive Collar

A defensive neckline technique is performed by buying an out-of-the-cash put choice and all the while composition an out-of-the-cash call alternative for the equivalent hidden resource and lapse. This procedure is frequently utilized by financial specialists after a long position in a stock has encountered considerable additions. This alternative blend enables financial specialists to have drawback security (long puts to secure benefits), while having the exchange off of conceivably being committed to sell shares at a more significant expense (selling higher = more benefit than at current stock levels). A straightforward model would be if a financial specialist is long 100 portions of IBM at $50 and IBM has ascended to $100 as of January 1. The speculator could develop a defensive neckline by selling one IBM March fifteenth 105 calls and all the while getting one IBM March 95 put. The merchant is secured beneath $95 until March 15; with the exchange off of possibly having the commitment to sell his/her offers at $105. In the P&L diagram, the defensive neckline is a blend of a secured call since a long time ago put. This is an impartial exchange set-up, implying that you are secured in case of falling stock, however with the exchange off of having the potential commitment to sell your long stock at the short call strike. Once more, however, the speculator ought to be glad to do as such, as they have just experienced gains in the hidden offers.

The Bear Put Spread

The bear put spread methodology is another type of vertical spread. In this procedure, the speculator will all the while buying put alternatives at a particular strike cost and sell a similar number of puts at a lower strike cost. The two choices would be for the equivalent basic resource and have a similar termination date. This system is utilized when the broker is bearish and expects the basic resource's cost to decrease. It offers both restricted misfortunes and constrained additions.

Joined Put

In a wedded put technique, a financial specialist buys an advantage (in this model, portions of stock), and all the while buys put choices for a proportional number of offers. The holder of a put alternative has the option to sell stock at the strike cost. The explanation of why a financial specialist would utilize this technique is essential to secure their drawback hazard when holding a stock. This system capacities simply like a protection strategy and builds up a value floor should the stock's value fall forcefully.

A case of a wedded put would be if a financial specialist purchases 100 portions of stock and gets one put the alternative at the same time. This procedure is engaging in light of the fact that a speculator is secured to the drawback should a negative occasion happen. Simultaneously, the speculator would take an interest in the majority of the upside if the stock gains in worth. The main drawback to this methodology happens if the stock doesn't fall; in which case, the financial specialist loses the premium paid for the put choice.

Secured Call

With calls, one system is essential to purchasing a stripped call alternative. You can likewise structure a fundamental secured call or purchase compose. This is a well-known methodology since it creates pay and decreases some danger of being long stock alone. The exchange off is that you should be eager to sell your offers at a set value: the short strike cost. To execute the technique, you buy the hidden stock as you regularly would, and at the same time, compose (or sell) a call choice on those equivalent offers.

In this model, we are utilizing a call alternative on a stock, which speaks to 100 portions of stock for each call choice. For every 100 portions of stock you get, you all the while sell 1 call alternative against it. It is alluded to as a shrouded call-in light of the fact that if a stock rocket higher in value, your short call is secured by the long stock position. Speculators may utilize this system when they have a transient situation in the stock and a nonpartisan feeling on its course. They may hope to create salary (through the clearance of the call premium), or secure against a potential decrease in the hidden stock's worth.

Develop a Trading Plan

A trading plan acts as a guide during your trading process. It is crucial to have one, especially if you want to earn huge profits from trading options. Below are some of the points to consider while making a trading plan:

<u>Set Goals</u>

If you want to succeed at something, you need to come up with a goal, target, or ambition that inspires you to work hard and accomplish what you are doing. As a beginner in the options trading industry, what change would you like to see in your life? Why would you like to trade options? Well, I'm sure that most people join this industry with the expectations of earning a fortune out of trading options.

Write down every goal that you have in mind and allow the goals to be a source of inspiration anytime you want to trade options. This ensures that you do not give up or lose hope in the process. You keep trading with the hope that things will get better, and you will achieve the dreams that you have.

Goals can be powerful tools that connect us to our future success.

<u>Know-How You Can Handle Success</u>

Eventually, when you become an expert trader, you are likely to earn high profits. How you utilize the income generated determines if you will keep earning more or you remain stagnant at one point. As a wise investor, you need to use your finances properly. You can utilize them well for the sake of future success.

This can involve reinvesting the income earned. By reinvesting, you keep earning more and more with each passing day. The good thing about options trading is that your earnings are not limited. You can trade as many times as you wish in a single day and earn big profits daily. When you master that art of trading options, it gets more comfortable with each day. You get to make huge profits effortlessly. However, while reinvesting, avoid using all the accumulated income.

Overconfidence can cause you to start making losses in options trading.

Know-How to Handle Failure

Like any other investment, one is bound to incur a loss or a profit. Profits are excellent, but losses are terrible nightmares. As a beginner, it is advisable that one takes up what one can handle.

If you are new to the option trading industry, avoid investing money that you cannot afford to lose. In the event, the trade goes contrary to what you anticipated; you will end up incurring huge losses. Each day we are having thousands of people joining options trading with high expectations. Some believe that it's an easy shortcut or way to get rich faster. Contrary to their belief, they have to put in a lot of effort to ensure that they can start earning from trading options.

Most of these diseases are caused by factors that we create on our own. An individual might be suffering from depression after making a big loss while trading options. This can be avoided by being prepared in case things do not move as expected.

Access Your Market Knowledge

Most people start trading options with very little knowledge of what it entails. As a result, they end up incurring huge losses since they lacked the required information. It's a good thing that you are already reading this book since it shows that you realize the importance of having information. Chances are, you will be highly equipped, unlike most people. The interesting fact about trading options is that there is something new to be learned on a daily basis. As the market expands and grows, more and more things are being discovered.

This allows you to know the best time to trade and also avoid trading when the market is not favorable. At the same time, you acquire some tips and tactics that enhance your trading skill, making you better than you were while beginning.

All the information is available on the internet and in books that you can easily access.

Know the Options Strategies

Option strategies form the basis of options trading. It goes with doubt that if you aspire to be an expert in options trading, you need to be aware of all the option strategies that you can utilize in a particular trade. Depending on the circumstances and factors surrounding a trade, different strategies will work in different situations. Some people are only aware of a few options strategies that they use in almost all the trades that they engage in. As a result, they end up making big losses, since the option strategies they used were not best suited for that trade.

This is a mistake most beginners make. In as much as you may be comfortable using a particular option strategy, you need to be fully aware of your other options. Ensure that you increase your knowledge for you to stand a better chance of succeeding at what you do. Once you are aware of all the strategies that you can utilize, you can easily make a trading plan. It allows you to know when to trade, when to hold and when not to trade at all.

Plan Your Entry and Exit

For one to be an expert in trading, they need to have a proper plan on when to exit and enter a trade. Some brokerage accounts provide graphs and analyses for the current options market. By analyzing the graphs, there is a lot of information that you can pick up. You get to evaluate the graph movements and look for signals that encourage you to enter a trade. Often, you get in a trade when the conditions around it are favorable, and the probability of succeeding in that particular trade is high.

When the conditions are not favorable or welcoming, it acts as a signal to avoid that particular trade so that you do not end up making a loss. Most people are good when it comes to the entry of a particular trade. Unfortunately, most do not know when to exit. As a result, they end up incurring losses, since they missed the exit signals.

The same way you analyze the graph to know the best time to enter a trade. Is the same way you should analyze it to know the best time to exit a trade.

This will save you from incurring losses.

Analyze Your Trading Progress

The best way to trace your trading progress is by writing down everything that you do. Have a journal where you write down your trading progress.

There are a lot of things that you will note once you start doing this. It allows you to know the best times you had while trading. You get to know the strategies that you utilized at that time, which led to your trading success. It allows you to see the trends and circumstances that resulted in a good and successful trade. All this information is relevant to your growth in the options trading industry. On the other hand, you become aware of the circumstances surrounding the unsuccessful trades that you might have had. It is also good to look at the amount of money you spent at various trades and how you were able to recover it after the trade. On the same note, look at the money that you lost.

Compare your success rates and your loss rates. See if the choices you are making are worth it.

This will help you grow in the options trading industry.

Establish Your Risk Tolerance

While trading options, you will come across both risks and rewards. Every trader aspires to get a reward while trading options. After all, the point of investing is to earn profits. No one likes to make a loss. We keep working hard and improving so that we can stand a better chance of succeeding in the options trading industry.

As a beginner or a person who is green in this field, there are a lot of factors that you will have to consider, especially if you want to make a living out of trading. It's not every day that you will be lucky while trading options, you will come across some bad days, where you make losses. Most people have a bad perception that options trading is a shortcut to getting rich. When you approach it with these perceptions, you will end up being frustrated. Like any other investment, options trading comes with its own risks. As a trader, you need to be aware of these risks and know how you will work your way around them to have a successful outcome.

Know what you can afford to lose so that you can determine what you can risk.

Have a Trading Routine

A trader needs to set a time when they can analyze the various trade movements. At times we invest in options trading blindly without analyzing the trade market. When things go contrary to what we expected, we end up concluding that options trading is a scam since we got nothing out of it. Well, the problem is that we do not take time to learn.

Spare some time to analyze your trades and get to see how you managed to succeed and what led to a loss, if at all, there was any. You also get to know the best time to carry out a trade and when to avoid carrying out a trade.

A routine will also help in tracking your progress.

Identify What to Trade

The options trading market is wide, and there are numerous trading parameters that you can decide to engage in. You could be a currency trader, stock trader, or join the other available trade markets. The decision you make entirely depends on you. However, before making that decision, it is important to equip yourself with all the necessary information regarding option markets.

Analyze the various markets to know what you can engage in and what to avoid engaging in. While studying, you will identify the pro and cons of the various markets. It is entirely up to you to know which market is worth spending your energy and finances on. Select a market that you are well conversant with and determine how you will succeed in that particular market. While making this decision, it is important to fully depend on yourself. What may have worked for your friend may not work for you. They may have chosen a market that they are well aware of, and if you make a mistake of choosing the same, you may end up making losses.

This process is very crucial and essential while trading options.

CHAPTER 12:

What Are Some Rules for Writing Covered Calls That a Trader Should Always Follow?

What is an Options Contract on the Stock Market?

The same thing happens in the stock market. Of course, in the case of the car, the buyer is simply hoping to get the car they want at what they perceive to be a bargain price, although if BMW really stopped making silver cars, they might sell it to a third party and then get a white one from the dealer. However, in most cases, the buyer wants the car. That isn't the case when it comes to options with stocks.

On the stock market, we are betting on the future price itself, and the shares of stock will be bought or sold at a profit if things work out. The key point is the buyer of the options contract is not hoping to acquire the shares and hold them for a long time period like a traditional investor.

Instead, you're hoping to make a bet on the price of the stock, secure that price, and then be able to trade the shares on that price no matter what happens on the actual markets. We will illustrate this with an example.

Call Options

A call is a type of options contract that provides the option to purchase an asset at the agreed-upon amount at the designated time or deadline. The reason you would do this is if you felt that the price of a given stock would increase in price over the specified time period. Let's illustrate with an example.

Suppose that Acme Communications makes cutting edge smartphones. The rumors are that they will announce a new smartphone in the next three weeks that is going to take the market by storm, with customers lined out the door to make preorders.

The current price that Acme Communications is trading at is $44.25 a share. The current pricing of an asset is termed as the spot price. Put another way; the spot price is the actual amount that you would be paying for the shares as you would buy them from the stock market right now.

Nobody really knows if the stock price will go up when the announcement is made, or if the announcement will even be made. But you've done your research and are reasonably confident these events will take place. You also have to estimate how much the shares will go up, and based on your research, you think it's going to shoot up to $65 a share by the end of the month.

You enter into an options contract for 100 shares at $1 per share. You pay this fee to the brokerage that is writing the options contract. In total, for 100 shares, you pay $100.

The price that is paid for an options contract is $100. This price is called the premium.

You don't get the premium back. It's a fee that you pay no matter what. If you make a profit, then it's all good. But if your bet is wrong, then you'll lose the premium. For the buyer of an options contract, the premium is their risk.

You'll want to set a price that you think is going to be lower than the level to which the price per share will rise. The price that you agree to is called the strike price. For this contract, you set your strike price at $50.

Remember, exercising your right to buy the shares is optional. You'll only buy the shares if the price goes high enough that you'll make a profit on the trade.

If the shares never go above $50, say they reach $48, you are not obligated to buy them. And why would you? As part of the contract deal, you'd be required to buy them at $50.

We'll say that the contract is entered on the 1st of August, and the deadline is the third Friday in August. If the price goes higher than your strike price during that time, you can exercise your option.

Let's say that as the deadline approaches, things go basically as you planned. Acme Communications announces its new phone, and the stock starts climbing. The stock price on the actual market (the spot price) goes up to $60.

Now the seller is required to sell you the shares at $50 a share. You buy the shares, and then you can immediately dispose of these at a quality or optimal amount, or $60 a share. You make a profit of $10 a share, not taking into account any commissions or fees.

Ways to Close an Options Contract

At the point when you purchase value alternatives, you truly have made no promise to purchase the fundamental value. Your alternatives are open. Here are three different ways to purchase choices with models that show when every strategy may be proper:

Hold until development…

…at that point exchange: This implies you clutch your choices contracts until the finish of the agreement time frame, before termination, and afterward practice the alternative at the strike cost.

When might you need to do this? Assume you were to purchase a Call alternative at a strike cost of $25, and the market cost of the stock advances consistently, moving to $35 toward the finish of the choice agreement time frame. Since the basic stock cost has gone up to $35, you would now be able to practice your Call alternative at the strike cost of $25 and advantage from a benefit of $10 per share ($1,000) before taking away the expense of the premium and commissions.

Exchange before the Termination Date

You practice your alternative sooner or later before the termination date.

For instance: You purchase a similar Call choice with a strike cost of $25, and the cost of the basic stock is fluctuating above and underneath your strike cost. Following half a month, the stock ascents to $31, and you don't figure it will go a lot higher, in reality, it could very well drop once more. You practice your Call alternative quickly at the strike cost of $25 and advantage from a benefit of $6 an offer ($600) before deducting the expense of the premium and commissions.

Allow the Alternative to Lapse

You don't exchange the choice and the agreement lapses.

Another model: You purchase a similar Call choice with a strike cost of $25, and the basic stock cost just stays there, or it continues sinking. You don't do anything. At termination, you will have no benefit, and the alternative will lapse useless. Your misfortune is restricted to the top-notch you paid for the choice and commissions.

Once more, in every one of the above models, you will have paid a premium for the alternative itself. The expense of the premium and any financier charges you paid will decrease your benefit. Fortunately, as a purchaser of alternatives, the premium and commissions are your solitary hazard. So, in the third model, although you didn't gain a benefit, your misfortune was constrained regardless of how far the stock value fell.

CHAPTER 13:

Strategies and Tricks That Can Be Applied

If you start using options for trading, you will feel bombarded with a lot of information. It is true. However, if you want to be motivated from the start and avoid these losses for beginners, you need to master some techniques to get started. Because in the final analysis, earnings/leverage is the only thing that can bring you benefits.

Although most people believe that there is indeed a "secret" that can keep the rich, and they cannot win other deals. But this is not far from the truth. All the secrets you will read here are common sense; it all depends on your ability to recognize and apply these contents.

The biggest secret of all (yes, even life) is patience and self-discipline. Every time you negotiate, you want to make sure you know something new, and that you're understanding of specific topics is constantly increasing. In this way, you will face challenges, but it is difficult and positive.

Never Think of Dollar Value. Consider a Fixed Percentage

This is one of the major mistakes that even middlemen make: they believe that the dollar amount they earn or assume in each transaction is high. If you think of the value of the U.S. dollar, you may want to earn at least $2 for every dollar you make in the trading account. Suppose you have a US$5,000 bill. Common sense says that you already have a $2 bet, which can happen in any way: it can be converted into profit or loss and also contains your original $1. Therefore, you decide to invest $500 in the game to earn $2 in profit for every $1. Simple calculations show that it only takes ten bad transactions to make money. On the other hand, considering these fixed percentages, clauses will take too much risk. Therefore, if you decide to risk 3% of the total capital to make money, you will only risk $150 per operation. Of course, this also means that the amount you can risk will increase as your account grows. Therefore, by thinking in terms of a fixed percentage rather than a dollar amount, major risks can be avoided.

Hedge

A hedge is one of the most important parts of trading options. For example, consider buying the opposite position and maintaining the current position. If you think the stock will rise, please buy only ten profitable options. But what if the universe is not good for you, but the action has not progressed? If the option expires, you will eventually lose money. But with underwriting, if the situation is unfavorable, you can turn your losses into profits by buying five sales options. So even if the situation is very bad, you can still make money. There is another coverage technology called coverage. In this technique, you own the underlying stock and sell the stock. Selling the purchased stock means that you agree to sell the stock at the strike price of the option. This means that your capital risk becomes an asset, which leads to a reduction in the funds lost in the event of development.

One thing to remember in every transaction is that you must use all the items in the arsenal and have as much influence as possible to make a profit. Use the different technologies and options you have. Similarly, take full advantage of the security gained from trading options.

There Has Never Been a "Multi-Purpose" Strategy

Regardless of market conditions, traders, and investors who follow a single strategy are usually people who are afraid of the stock market. Unless fundamentals change significantly, they will continue to invest rather than sell. If you want to make a profit quickly and avoid long-term risks, it is completely wrong.

Also, the "multi-purpose" strategy has never been used like some operators. In this case, you must follow the process and adjust to the market. Conditions allow market conditions to guide you in the right direction. More, you will leave profitably. This means that you will never forget the opportunity to buy call options, spreads, and put options. But of course, before buying, you need to understand what is happening in the market. This is where research comes into play.

There is Always an Exit Strategy

It must happen self-evidently. You should always walk on corners and develop exit strategies. It doesn't matter if you win or lose. A good exit strategy can help you minimize losses when problems occur. Also, it can help you get rid of some transactions that can still make money. On the other hand, exit strategies can also prevent you from losing profits in the future. This rule is universal for any type of investment. You need to make sure you can get out of trouble with a smile and a healthy mood.

Conduct Research before Repeating

If you know that a business is going according to plan, it is easy to double your profits. But bad things can happen. You find trends and then act accordingly to avoid losses. Make sure you know that the trend is strong, and you can trust it to make a profit. Even after that, when things go south, you still need to make an exit plan to save yourself. Do not accompany you when it comes to trading options, because your account will eventually be destroyed. It may be easy to open a new trading account, but it is not worth it. In the beginning, you should try to climb down and learn to make ropes, then gradually increase the risk. Over time, you will be able to lead a business lifestyle.

Never Use Cashless Redemption Options (ATM) to Start Trading

This appears to be the right approach, but the more option is to reduce the exchange. Buying cheap and selling expensive is a good thing because that is the business/business mentality that all of us have. But you will see that trading options are much more than buying at a low price and selling at a high price. You can use many other means to increase profits continuously.

ATM calling is one of the biggest mistakes that make beginners choose to trade. They do not know that this is one of the most difficult ways to make money at a constant level.

What's wrong with buying a phone?

It takes a lot of research and resistance to determine the trend of the stock. Not only must you determine the direction correctly, but you must also determine the direction correctly. If something goes wrong, you will lose the royalties paid for this option. Moreover, when things go south, just by sitting in the sun, the movement will not move in the desired direction every day. You are waiting for the deadline every day because there is not much to do.

In this case, to make an informed transaction, all you can do is sell ATM calls on stocks you already own. In terms of options traded, this is called the "call option." What you basically agree with is that if the strike price is higher than the current stock price and the stock price reaches or exceeds the strike price during the above period, there is no obligation to sell the stock to the buyer in the name. In this way, you can make money by selling ATM calls. If the stock price reaches the highest price, you will get more profits.

Selling your ATM calls can reduce risk and put it into practice. This means that, despite the high risk, if you do not sell so-called ATMs, you will not lose so much money. Nonetheless, when the stock price hits the target price, and the economy stays stable, you will not lose much, and you will be charged a sales premium. Eventually, you will be able to sell ATM calls for a long time.

By contrast, if you are familiar with the world of options by selling guaranteed calling options, you will learn the queue faster without losing a lot of money. It is considered wise to sell covered phones strategy, because the risk is very low, and you can still make a considerable profit.

In addition, you will learn how option prices respond to small fluctuations in stocks and how prices fall over time.

Options with Poor Trading Liquidity

If you want to profit quickly, liquidity is important. Liquidity means that the market is ready, and buyers and sellers have been active. The mathematical definition of liquidity is the probability that the next transaction will be executed at a price equal to the last one. In addition to options trading, stock exchanges are usually more liquid. This is because stock traders trade only one type of stock. In contrast, options traders have a large number of contracts to choose from. For example, stock traders only need to buy one form of IBM stock.

On the other hand, options traders have many expiration dates and many strike prices to choose from. This means that the options market is not as liquid as the stock market. But IBM has nothing to do with options trading or liquidity in the stock market.

Let us give another example of a company smaller than IBM. Compared with IBM, higher processing inventory will be more inactive, while options will be more inactive. Superior Processors is a fictitious processing enterprise that promises that the world will use quantum processors within five years. Since this is a small company, its stock is only traded once a week and can only be traded by appointment.

When the stock is inactive, the buying and selling price of the option is artificially increased. For example, if the buy and sell margin is 0.30 USD (buy price = 1.90 USD, buy = 2.20 USD), and if you buy the contract at 2.20 USD, you will immediately establish a loss position. Also, due to the lack of liquidity in the market for this particular operation, you will also need to solve many problems. When you start trading options, the best thing you can do is to trade liquid options. It will not only save you a lot of time, resources, and stress, but you can also learn a lot in a short time.

Options Trading Mistakes to Avoid

Options trading is entirely different from regular stock exchange investing. Let's think for a moment about the common wisdom that is dispensed concerning stock exchange investing. The overall idea is to buy and hold, keeping your investments for an extended period. You are expected to keep your assets until retirement. People do various strategies, like rebalancing their portfolio to match their goals, diversification, and dollar-cost averaging.

Options trading is a different way of watching things. First of all, even if you are a day trader or engaging in swing trading activities, the overall goal, when it involves stocks, is to buy when the price is at a comparatively low point then sell at a high price. The day trader, the swing trader, and the buy-and-hold investor are not any different. Buy-and-hold investors think that they are unique and above everyone else; they are, actually, just trying to make money off the stock exchange too. The only real difference, unless you are a dividend investor, is the timeframe involved. So, your buy-and-hold investor goes to carry the stocks for 25 years; then, they are going to start cashing them out for money. A swing trader makes money in the here and now.

<u>Going into a Trade Too Big</u>

One of the mistakes that people make when they start options trading is making their positions too big. Since our options don't cost all that much compared to stocks' prices, people aren't used to trading in smaller amounts. People who are not rich, thinking of the stock price and how much 100 shares value. This way will set up people for trouble. The temptation will be there to move on a large number of contracts once you start making your trades if you have the capital to buy or sell them. This manner will get people into trouble. It is not the dollar amount that is a priority, but it could put you in a position where you cannot act as quickly as you possibly need to depend on the situation. If you discover a trade and choose to sell 20 contracts if the trade goes south, trying to buyback those 20 contracts could be problematic. Or you might find yourself buying a bunch of call options and have trouble getting out of them on the same day.

It's better to have a couple of different small positions with the options than to have multiple positions once they are large. Remember that options prices move fast. You don't want to over-leverage your trades and be in a place where you cannot find a buyer to pick up all 10 or 20 contracts.

Not Paying Attention to Expiration

This fact is probably one of the most common mistakes made by beginning traders. The expiration date is one of the most important factors that should be considered when you enter your trades. And once you have entered a business, you need to have the expiration date of the option tattooed on your forehead. This fact is often something that is not amenable to being ignored. First of all, choosing the expiration date when entering the position is as important as picking the options' strike price. But one of the things that beginners do is to focus too much on the price of the option and the price-setting for the strike. The value of the option and the strike price is essential; the expiration date is critical also.

Buying Cheap Options

There is a proverb that says you get what you pay for. There are reasons to buy out of the money options sometimes, but you shouldn't go too far out of the money. Unfortunately, many beginning traders are tempted to go far out of the money for the sake of buying a low-priced option. The matter with these options is that even though out of the cash options can make profits. If they are too far out of the money, they are not going to see any action. There is no sense in buying an inexpensive option because you can pick it up for $25. You do not want to be sinking your money into options where a huge price move would be necessary to earn any profits. It is fine to buy options that are near the capital. Options on the brink of being in the money are often very profitable even though they are out of the money. If you are looking to save lots of a little bit of money when starting your investing, that is always something to think about. But to make profits, the essential rule is there has got to be some reasonable chance that the stock prices will move enough to make the choice you buy worth the money.

Failing to Close When Selling Options

If you need to recollect only one thing from our conversation about selling options, whether it is selling put credit spreads or naked puts, you should keep in mind that it is always possible to exit the trade. The way that you leave the business once you sell to open is your buy to close. You need to take care of doing this because it is too easy to give in to your emotions and panic, and prematurely exit a trade. However, it would help if you remembered the likelihood of closing the business in the least times. Riding out an option to expiration may be a foolish move unless it is very clear that it will expire out of the money.

As a part of this problem, new options traders often come to the market, focusing on hope as a strategy. When it involves investing, hope is certainly not a strategy. Hope is some things that belong to a casino playing coin machine games. When you are training options, you ought to take as rational a choice as you will make given the circumstances. So, when the expiration date is closing, it is clear that the trade will not be profitable, do not concede to the temptation to talk about waiting around for a reversal in direction. Once you say something like that to yourself, which exposes the temptation to remain in the trade far too long. At some point, you would possibly not be able to recover at all. So, what you do not want to do, which is often correct buying and selling, is hoping that there will be a turnaround and waiting to see what happens.

Trading Illiquid Options

This option is such a crucial issue I will repeat it. Liquidity is significant when trading options. What liquidity means is the ability to buy and sell financial security quickly and switch it into cash. It is not enough to love the corporate to start trading options on the company. If the open interest for an option is merely 8, 10, or maybe 45, that will present obstacles once you need to move to get rid of an option fast. The most important companies generally have liquid options, but you ought to always check. Index funds even have liquid options. Avoid any companies that have small open interests. The only way that you would trade when the open interest exists with little is if the probability of losing out on the trade is minuscule. So, besides the strike price, share price, an expiration date, you need to be looking closely at open interest. You do not want to get in a situation where you cannot exit a position.

Not Having a Trading Plan

One of the best things about options trading is that it is elementary. So, you have this relatively low-cost way to become involved in the stock market, and it is also relatively easy to manage on your own. These are positives generally speaking, but there is a downside. That downside is that the indisputable fact that it is very easy for people just to start trading on a whim. Make no mistake, because it is easy that doesn't mean the cash and potential losses aren't real. So, you need to treat this with the utmost seriousness. Take a while to develop a trading plan. The trading plan should include many of the things we mentioned earlier, like the extent of profit that you are willing to accept any trade. It should also set up a limit that is used to determine when to exit your positions. But I forgot to say one important thing. Your trading plan should also detect a maximum of 5 financial securities that you will focus on when trading options. In my opinion, doing more than five financial securities is more than your mind can handle. I say that you should be keeping close watching over each of the businesses for index funds that you were trading. If you have more than five, that is not going to be possible. And as I've said before, one of the things about options trading is that the pricing can move very quickly. So, if you are trying to spread your attention in 20 different directions, you are likely to lose money because you cannot keep track of everything.

Failing to Have an Exit Plan

You should have an exit plan for each one of your trades. I like better to have an overall exit plan and have every business follow the same basic rules. An exit plan will assist you in minimizing your losses. This fact goes back to the matter of beginning traders holding onto an option until the expiration date. That is more likely to happen if you have not formulated a strategy to exit your position. It may help keep a notebook to record all of your trades and write down every transaction's principles. That way, you can consult it when things are fluctuating, possibly putting you into a situation where there are catastrophic losses. Of course, they are not disastrous, assuming that you are reasonable in the number of options contracts that you trade one move. But you need to have some rule to exit the trade if the losses exceed a particular amount. Of course, sometimes, you are going to make an error. So, in other words, if you have some kind of rules like you are going to sell to close if the loss reaches $50, something I can guarantee is at some point, you are going to do this, but the stock goes to rebound, and if you had stayed in, you would have made $200 or something like that. You only need to accept that, sometimes, if you will miss out on situations like that. But on average, that is not likely to happen. So, if an option goes south and you have a $50 exit rule, it is a good idea only to follow it and accept the results.

CHAPTER 14:

Has Anyone Made Any Significant Money from Trading?

Ensuring dependable profits in the financial markets is much more difficult than it seems at first glance. It is assessed that over 75% of all members, in the end, wash out and take up more secure side interests. Be that as it may, the financier business once in a while distributes customer disappointment rates, since they're concerned reality may drive away new records, so the washout rate could be a lot higher.

The Road to Long-Term Profitability

Long haul benefit requires two interrelated ranges of abilities. To begin with, we need techniques that get more cash-flow than they lose. Second, those techniques must perform well while the market shape-moves through bull and bear driving forces, with a lot of uneven periods in the middle. While numerous brokers realize how to profit in explicit economic situations, similar to a solid upturn, they bomb over the long haul because their techniques don't adjust to unavoidable changes.

So, would you be able to split away from the pack and unite the expert minority with a methodology that raises your chances for long haul success? Begin with an unmistakable and succinct arrangement.

<u>Disregard the Holy Grail</u>

Losing brokers fantasize about the mystery recipe that will mysteriously improve their outcomes. Connect with Your Trading Plan

Update your trading plan week by week or month to month to incorporate new thoughts and kill awful ones. Return and read the arrangement at whatever point you fall in an opening and are searching for an approach to get out.

Be Careful with Reinforcement

Dynamic trading discharges adrenaline and endorphins. These synthetics can create sentiments of happiness notwithstanding when you are losing cash. Thus, this urges addictive characters to take terrible positions, just to get the hurry.

Try Not to Cut Corners

Your opposition burns through many hours of consummating methodologies and you are in for a severe shock in the event that you hope to toss a couple of darts and leave with a benefit.

Grasp Simplicity

Concentrate on value activity, understanding that everything else is optional. Feel free to assemble complex specialized markers yet remember their essential capacity is to affirm or disprove what you're prepared eye as of now observes.

Evade the Obvious

Benefit infrequently pursues the greater part. When you see an ideal exchange arrangement, almost certainly, every other person sees it too, planting you in the group and setting you up for disappointment.

Arrange Your Personal Life

Whatever is not right in your life will in the end persist into your trading execution. This is particularly risky on the off chance that you haven't profited, riches and the attractive extremity of plenitude and shortage.

Try Not to Break Your Rules

You make trading principles to get you out of inconvenience when positions go seriously. On the off chance that you don't enable them to carry out their responsibility, you have lost your order and opened the entryway to significantly more noteworthy misfortunes.

Tune in to Your Intuition

Trading utilizes the scientific and imaginative sides of your cerebrum, so you have to develop both to prevail over the long haul. When you are alright with math, you can upgrade results with reflection, a couple of yoga stances, or a tranquil stroll in the recreation center.

Make Peace with Losses

Trading is one of only a handful couple of callings where losing cash each day is a characteristic way to progress. Each trading misfortune accompanies a significant market exercise in case you are available to the message.

Try Not to Believe in a Company

In case you are excessively enamored with your trading vehicle, you offer an approach to defective basic leadership. You must gain by wastefulness, profiting while every other person is inclining the incorrect way.

Lose the Crowd

Long haul productivity requires situating in front of or behind the group, yet never in the group since that is the place savage techniques target. Avoid stock sheets and visit rooms. This is not kidding business and everybody in those spots has an ulterior thought process.

Try Not to Try to Get Even

Drawdowns are a characteristic piece of the merchant's life cycle. Acknowledge them effortlessly and adhere to the reliable methodologies you realize will in the long run recover your presentation on track.

Try Not to Count Your Chickens

Like an exchange that is going your direction, yet the cash is not yours until you closeout.

Watch for Early Warnings

Huge misfortunes once in a while happen without various specialized admonitions. Dealers routinely overlook those signs and would like to supplant keen control, setting themselves up for torment.

Apparatuses Don't Think

Dealers compensate for deficient aptitudes with costly programming, prepackaged with a wide range of exclusive purchase and sell signals. These apparatuses meddle with important experience since you think the product is more brilliant than you are.

Play with Your Head

It's normal for dealers to copy their monetary saints but at the same time, it's an ideal method to lose cash. Take in what you can from others, at that point back off, and set up your very own market personality, in light of your one-of-a-kind abilities and risk resistance.

Jettison the Paycheck Mentality

We're educated to pound through the stir week and afterward get our checks. This compensation for-exertion remunerate mindset clashes with the common progression of trading wins and misfortunes over the span of a year. Truth be told, insights show that most yearly benefits are set up for only a bunch of days the market is open for business.

Conclusion

Options trading is different from other forms of financial markets, but if you have experience trading shares, stock, Forex and other forms of trading, it will be of help. You can use the experience of other forms of financial instruments to predict the market so it will be easier for those with these experiences.

However, the newbie with little or no experience in the financial market can pick up easily and start trading as soon as possible. They just need to pick up the basics of options trading, the basic terminology and learn how to place orders with options. We should remember that the option is a time base contract, and our profit or loss is registered at the end of the contract. However, we still sell the contract before it expires to minimize our loss or make a profit in the market.

One area the inexperienced traders should focus on is the process of taking orders in the market; they have to spend time learning the basic terminologies and what they stand for and how to use these terms. They have to grasp the use of technical and fundamental indicators to open options and follow up on the trades so they can minimize their losses and make a profit. If you have traded Forex or shares, then these analyses will be convenient for you, and options will be easier for you as you get familiar with the terms. But the newbie will have to take deep courses in reading charts with fundamental and technical analyses.

The brokers you use are very important in helping you to become a good trader. There are brokers who will provide help to newbie's and make them become a decent trader, while some are more focused on experienced traders. In summary, you should select the broker that meets up the requirement as a trader to be able to grow and become a better trader.

Trading options can give you higher returns than other forms of financial instruments. And that is why more people are getting interested in trading options. But you will require the right knowledge to be able to trade it successfully. A good strategy and patience are required in the market, and this has seen many people fail and lost several accounts on trading options. Do not make the mistake of viewing options as a bet, where you can put your money on any position without proper analyzes of the market.

Option trading goes beyond learning the strategies, taking profits, and maintaining losses.

Trading psychology has become popular over the years as it is believed the way we behave and react to news determine our success in the market. So, we need to get it right, not only with our attitude towards trading but also with our mindset.

Making money is a continuous process, and one has to be consistent with what you are doing. And our main aim as a trader is to make money continuously. Although no plan can guarantee you 100% with financial trading but with consistency, you can actually grow your account.

There are people making a living out of options trading, and this is due to the consistency in their trade. It is not that they do not register losses, but their success rate is more than their losses, and they have a good money management system.

A good management system should not have your account depleted in half after just a few losses. When you have a good management system, losses will not get you upset at the market; rather, you will pick up easily because you know your account cannot be affected by that loss. But when you have bad management, any loss will have a huge impact on your account, and a few losses will ruin your account.

It takes time to become profitable in trading, and your first few months may not go as you will expect. The process of trading is a continuous learning process, and you have to research all the time to improve your trading. It will do you a great deal if you have a mentor, someone you can look up to, especially when there consistent bad days in the market.

A mentor will encourage you and give you the zeal to continue with your quest. I will advise you not to view trading as a means of making money. Take it as a science or art of learning the market, and this will give you a different view of trading. When entering the market each day, do not think of how much you are going to make, but about how many trades you are going to get right.

You should view the market from successful trade and not making money. With good management of your account, 7 out of 10 successful trades will put you in a good place of making money. And that should be our aim in options trading, to get a high proportion of successful trade to losses.

OPTIONS TRADING STRATEGIES

In the market, you have to know when to hold an asset and when to let them go. When you let go of an asset either in profit or in loss, you will be managing the profit as well as minimizing your loss. Do not compound loss, and if your readings tell you the market is not getting better, and then cut your losses. The same goes for when you are in a profit, by taking an analysis of the market, you can determine that the market or trend is coming to an end and take your profit.

In trading, you are going to find yourself in the process and choose what is good for you. Take your time to get the feel of trading, and it will come to you. With trading, you will discover yourself as you learn more about discipline and other personal attributes that will affect your lifestyle.

About the Author

My name is Nathan Price born in 1983 in New York. I live in Shanghai near Wall Street with my family. My love for mathematics started when I was a child and as I grew up, I channeled my passion for economics and finance and ended up studying finance and investment. As a financial analyst, I have traveled around the world but mostly in Europe and Asia. Today I am one of the biggest financial analysts as I work for a large trading company in New York. I have been in the trading market for over 10 years and my job focuses on the research of methods and strategies you can use to make money investing in options, stocks, currencies, cryptocurrencies, and many more.

I am an advocate of trading and I teach people to become less dependent on their monthly salaries and try investing. I don't regret joining the trade market and I am sure that you will not regret it too.

I have a family to take care of and cash flow that is enough to cover everything after retirement. I am happy to be with them during this period. For me, a family is the most important thing; it is a place to return. I wish to follow my passion, my dreams because if I fulfill myself with happiness, I will share it with my family.

I am a well-respected author who writes books that help those in need of positive changes in their lives or the lives of their loved ones. My passion in life is to help enlighten those who are searching for answers to help them live a better and more productive life.

I offer free blog articles with weekly subscriptions via my website (For you)

I enjoy traveling, making money, socializing, meeting new people, and helping them improve their investment life.

You Can Also connect with me on...

Twitter: (For you)

Blog: (For you)

Facebook: (For you)

LinkedIn: (For you)

Other Books by Nathan Price: (For you)

Made in the USA
Monee, IL
08 May 2021